# How to Start Making Money with your Sewing

## Karen Maslowski

**BETTERWAY BOOKS**
CINCINNATI, OHIO

# About the Author

Karen Maslowski is the author of *Sew Up A Storm: All the Way to the Bank!* and the editor of *Sew Up A Storm: The Newsletter for Sewing Entrepreneurs*. She has sewn for others and taught sewing for many years, and regularly appears at sewing shows, lecturing about sewing as a business. Karen and her family live in Cincinnati, Ohio.

02  01  00  99  98      5  4  3  2  1

**Library of Congress Cataloging-in-Publication Data**

Maslowski, Karen
 How to start making money with your sewing / by Karen
Maslowski. —1st ed.
     p.     cm.
 Includes index.
 ISBN 1-55870-474-4 (pbk.)
 1. Clothing trade—Management. 2. Dressmaking. 3. New business
enterprises—Management. I. Title.
HD9942.A2M37   1998
646.4'068'1—dc21                                           97-49011
                                                                CIP

Edited by David Borcherding
Production edited by Michelle Howry
Cover designed by Cathleen Shaw

# Table of Contents

# Introduction

But yield who will to their separation,
My object in living is to unite
My avocation and my vocation
As my two eyes make one in sight.

From *Two Tramps in Mud Time* by Robert Frost

Home-based businesses are one of the fastest growing areas of the U.S. economy. One study estimated there were over eighteen million home-based businesses in this country as of early 1997. Of these, about one-fourth of them focus on personal services or creative design, such as sewing.

Perhaps you already belong to or are tempted to join this growing army of the self-employed. It's only natural to want to use your talents and favorite activities to make money. Sewing skills were once a part of life in nearly every home but are now much less common and becoming increasingly marketable. Many sewing enterprises have begun with a talented seamstress helping nonsewing friends and relatives. By identifying the need for such skills in your community, you have taken the first step toward creating a successful sewing business.

However, a sewing-business owner has an awful lot of hats to wear: contractor, financier, designer, accountant, buyer, marketer and tax specialist—to name just a few. How does a person who loves to sew keep the business productive and profitable—goods flowing out, money coming in—without losing the artistic, creative flair that inspired the business in the first place?

To fulfill your dreams you need to have more than just a good idea and a desire to create. You also need the skills to market your service or product, the ability to develop your particular market niche, and the flexibility to change your business to fit both your needs and the needs of the market.

This book is a compilation of the combined business experience of several successful sewing entrepreneurs, plus all new information on the latest in machines, computers and pricing. I hope to help you smoothly conquer the learning curve of a fledgling sewing business so that you can successfully unite *your* vocation and avocation!

CHAPTER 1

# How to Know if It's Time to Turn Your Hobby Into a Business

Everyone knows how well you sew. People ask you how much you would charge to make that dress for them. Or that crib blanket. Or that window treatment. Or one of your unique craft items. Is this the time to begin that sewing business you've had in the back of your mind for awhile? Maybe it is. Let's examine all the possibilities.

## Questions to ask yourself

- Are your sewing skills up-to-date?
- What sewing specialty interests you?
- Is there a strong market for this specialty?
- What kind of local competition exists?
- Are you confident of your ability to own a business?
- Are you confident of the concept you've designed?
- Can you sustain your interest in the business long enough to succeed?
- Are you ready to lose your hobby?

## Are your sewing skills up-to-date?

Perhaps you have sewn all your life. You're fairly confident of your ability to sew for yourself, but what about sewing for others? Before you take on the responsibility of starting a sewing business, you must first carefully evaluate your skills and knowledge in the field.

Are you up-to-date in the latest methods and fabrics? What are the latest trends in your area of expertise? If you have a desire to do dressmaking, are you able to fit any type of body style? And what about your knowledge of patterns? Are you willing to learn to create your own pat-

2

terns, or can you change existing patterns to suit your customers' needs? If you've chosen to create custom window treatments, are you current with the latest styles in this ever-changing field? If you wish to make quilts, how is your spatial ability? Can you determine which colors are most pleasing with one another?

These are important considerations. If you feel unsure about your sewing skills, this is the time to update your training. Taking some refresher classes at consumer shows may help, or perhaps more comprehensive training in your field is in order. Many professional organizations offer classes, seminars and other training resources to keep you current with the latest techniques and trends in your field.

Joining a professional sewing group is another way to develop your sewing skills and meet like-minded professionals. Being able to discuss difficult situations and share common experiences helps everyone—you, the others in the group and eventually your clients. If there isn't such a group in your area, you might want to start one. See the appendix for more information on sewing groups and other valuable training resources.

If you aren't confident of how well you can sew, your customer won't be either. A quiet assurance that you know what you're doing will go a long way toward easing many customer objections.

# What sewing specialty interests you?

Are you turned off by the idea of sewing window treatments but fascinated by the intricacies of lovely beaded wedding creations? Or does the thought of creating a custom-designed dress for someone appeal to you? If you are drawn to one kind of sewing, think of how you can develop this into a business. Is there a market for your wonderfully original, hand-sewn teddy bears? Has the experience of moving frequently given you excellent skills in dressing windows? Or has your frugal practice of re-covering your furniture given you an interest in doing slipcovers?

Think about what type of sewing particularly appeals to you. Having a specialty area, or two or three, helps your business succeed where others may fail. There are many reasons for specializing, which will be discussed in chapter two.

# James Powell

**Powell Manufacturing Industries, Inc.**
**Washington, DC**

"It all began with a string. Someone had given me a string of cotton fiber and told me that I should try to figure out a way to make a business out of it. It was a challenge that kept my mind going for months," says James Powell. He had been downsized from his government job, and for several months he researched possible business ideas he could implement himself. One aspect of his severance package included the accrued value of his retirement program; James planned to use this money to start his business.

After more than two months of pondering what to do with that string, James saw someone using a mop to clean the lobby of a nearby office building. He suddenly realized how he could use that string to create a business—he would manufacture and sell cotton fiber mops.

First, James did a market study. He wanted to know how many cleaning companies there were in the Washington, DC, area. Another important statistic was the number of public buildings, apartment buildings and private homes in the vicinity. Once he had determined that a market existed for his cotton fiber mops, James put together a business plan. After discussing the plan with his wife, Rebecca, he took a deep breath and withdrew his retirement money.

Because mops need to be sewn to their bases, James bought an industrial-strength sewing machine and taught himself to sew. But it was a frustrating experience. "I broke about 1,500 needles—the repairman became my best friend," James remembers. "He finally asked me to sew while he was watching, and he realized he needed to explain to me that the feed dogs pull the fabric past the needle. I was pushing it along, which is why the needles kept breaking." This didn't slow James down, though—he practiced twenty to thirty minutes a night to get the rhythm of sewing down pat.

In addition to training, James found that starting a sewing business required ingenuity and problem-solving skills. Because mops are sold by weight rather than by size, he designed a machine to "manicure" the mops—to trim them so each conformed to the specified weight. Along with this machine and the sewing stations, James worked out an assembly line, moving from the raw materials to shipping the finished goods out the door.

After he had his product design and the operations all figured out, James had to find a larger market. His first attempt was to make a bid on a contract for the DC public schools. Winning the bid proved to be a Catch-22—he needed the lucrative account but couldn't produce the necessary two thousand mops by himself. Because he was still working alone, James had to buy the mops from another company in Georgia. By the time he'd been in business eight or nine months, he was ready to hire his first employee.

One of the lessons James has learned from his business is that persistence pays off. When he contacted Joan Henderson, a buyer for the local grocery chain Giant Foods, she invited James to meet her. Though she said Giant had no business for his company at that time, she told him to stay in touch. James took her literally.

Every Wednesday at 10:00 A.M. he called her. "After about three months, she knew it would be my call at that time," he says. "I would say 'Good morning, Ms. Henderson,' and she would answer, 'Good morning, Mr. Powell,' every week." Finally Ms. Henderson made an initial order, for ten dozen mops a month. This business has grown to an average order of forty dozen mops a week. "Giant Foods nurtured my business; when I could produce more,

they ordered more, " says Powell of this business partnership. Currently his company has eight full-time employees and four to five seasonal hires.

James Powell has this advice for businesspeople: "The margins are better in manufacturing than in custom work, so look into that aspect of your business. Be relentless in your pursuit of whatever you want to do; you have to be obsessed by a dream. Work hard, but smart. Be willing to deny yourself; I worked seven days a week for four years before I could relax a little. Never give up. Rest—you *need* to rest—but don't quit. I want to inspire people to be producers instead of consumers."

# Is there a strong market for this specialty?

This is a key consideration, and one on which your success will depend heavily. One frustrated seamstress told me she had a fantasy of owning a dressmaking business. But her small town just didn't have the clients to support such a specialized enterprise. A more realistic approach is to make a match between your interests and skills, and the needs of your community.

For example, you may find there is a strong market for altering ready-to-wear clothing in your town, but little call for custom work. On the other hand, perhaps your city is experiencing a surge in new home construction; this could create a great demand for window treatments and other home decor items. Because many industries are calling for more casual work clothing, only bigger cities are good markets for career wear right now.

Perhaps your specialty isn't dependent on the local market. Some of the entrepreneurs profiled in this book are creating goods for the national or international market. Even if you live in a remote or rural area, you can have a successful business if you choose your specialty wisely.

# What local competition exists?

If you live in a small town that already has three bridal shops, this obviously wouldn't be the wisest choice for your specialty. But maybe there's a need for alterations on ready-to-wear gowns, or perhaps you would prefer to cater to the needs of the family after the wedding. Are children's clothes readily available? Is anyone else making slipcovers? Is there a product that is popular locally (garden flags, cement goose clothing, mailbox covers, horse blankets) that isn't being made by anyone else?

The key is to identify where you can compete in your local market. If the dry cleaner down the street charges so little for its customers' alterations that you just can't compete, a better choice might be to change your specialty to something else. Another example of this problem is the production of bridesmaids' gowns—an area where many beginning sewing businesses cut their prices substantially in an attempt to undercut prices at local shops. It's almost impossible to compete in this business atmosphere, and my advice is not to even try. Let others lose money doing such work for little pay; it simply isn't worth the aggravation to make $75 (or less) a dress. In most communities this price would cause the dressmaker to lose money. If you can't make a profit in a particular segment of the market, choose another specialty.

# Are you confident of your ability to own a business?

As I said in the introduction to this book, there are more considerations to having a successful sewing business than knowing how to sew well. If you feel you have a need for more knowledge in general business subjects, there are some great resources available. Your local Extension Agency may have classes specific to a sewing business. Service Corps of Retired

Executives (SCORE), a volunteer offshoot of the Small Business Administration (SBA), may have a volunteer on staff who can help you. If none is available at the moment, don't hesitate to check again later. The service is free and can be invaluable in helping you identify the strengths and weaknesses of your business ideas.

# Are you confident of the concept you've designed?

One pitfall in starting a new business is that others around you will test your resolve; they may even try to put obstacles in your path to success. If you have firm assurance and confidence in your plan, these obstacles will melt away, along with the objections family members or friends might have to your ambitions and dreams.

Again, here is where some expert advice can help. If you plan to offer concierge service alterations to office buildings but are too shy to present the program to concierge managers, it probably won't work very well. And if you don't think it will actually be to their benefit, you're sure to fail. There are some terrific motivational tapes and books that can help you overcome your own fears. Any library or bookstore will have such resources; avail yourself of all the help you can get.

If you sense there might be objections to your new business, keep your plans to yourself for awhile, at least until they have enough strength to sustain themselves in your mind. There's no substitute for a burning desire or ambition! If you are driven to accomplish a goal or to create a plan for yourself, you can't help but succeed.

# Can you sustain your interest in the business long enough to succeed?

Consider this scenario: You decide to make three hundred teddy bears to sell at shows. By the time you have finished them, you're so tired of seeing fur all over the place you never want to even hear the words *teddy bear* again! Can you make a business of this, or would it be better for you to make more of a variety of products to sell?

Likewise, do you enjoy doing alterations enough to make a business of them? Can you stand being around interior designers who want you to change designs all the time? Or do you want to voluntarily place yourself in the way of a bride whose weight is fluctuating wildly the last few weeks before her wedding, or whose mother may be forcing the daughter to accept a wedding that fulfills *her* desires?

Look ahead to see how you feel about recreating any one activity for an extended period of time.

# Are you ready to lose your hobby?

A "hobby" is fun; "work" isn't. It's as simple as that. If you turn your hobby into a moneymaking enterprise, will it still be fun for you? For some people it is a dream come true to do something they love all day long. For others, it's a nightmare. Why? Because they no longer have the time or the inclination to enjoy the activity just for fun. Before you spend any more time on planning a business, this is something to consider carefully.

For Karen Howland, a couture bridal designer in Chillicothe, Illinois, her once-favorite hobby is still a wonderful, enjoyable business pursuit. However, she has changed her attitude toward sewing considerably in the fifteen years or so she has sewn for the public. When she wants to relax now, she switches to knitting, also a longtime hobby. Knitting is a pleasure because it's totally for herself; there's no client input as to design, color or style, and Karen can create to her heart's content.

Before you decide to commit yourself to weekly work activity that you used to enjoy for fun, decide how you feel about this. Are you willing to relegate your own projects to the back burner, or do you hope to fit them in during your workday? Any time you aren't sewing for others you aren't making money; is this OK with you?

# Deborah Jackson

Sewing Services
Fairfield, Ohio

Debby Jackson loves to make the same thing over and over, the more the better. She likes the "mindless" repetition of not having to think about what comes next. Her business, Sewing Services, specializes in contract and production sewing. She and her employees make thousands of the same item for each of their customers, which means creativity is almost nonexistent in their work life.

Sewing Services makes uniform shirts and aprons for grocery store chains and restaurants. One of Debby's specialties is maternity uniform pants; her company inserts the stretchy panels into hundreds of premade slacks. Because of the limited need for this item, the large uniform companies don't want to retool their entire line for this small segment of their customers. Instead, they subcontract the work to someone like Debby, who can more easily handle these "smaller" quantities.

While this type of work suits Deborah Jackson just fine, for some it wouldn't be any fun at all. By identifying her own personal strengths and preferences, she has built a successful business with the sewing she enjoys.

CHAPTER 2

# Specialize!

In my book *Sew up a Storm: All the Way to the Bank!*, I identified seventy different sewing specialties, and there are many more ways to make money with sewing. Already in this book, I have referred to several ideas, but there are almost limitless opportunities.

Look around you; notice what the sewn products are everywhere. In a catalog of novelty goods, you'll find stuffed toys, home decor items, specialty clothing, garden items, all manner of giftware, household helpers, table decorations and so much more. Driving down a city street, you'll observe awnings, streetlight banners, flags, display props, even the "headlight bra" on the front of that foreign car! Further investigation will reveal boat covers, sails, motorcycle packs, bicycle flags, kites, hot-air balloons, backpacks and on and on. Ideas abound.

# Why should you specialize?

There are lots of good reasons to specialize. The first, and best, one is that there are vast pricing differences between various sewing disciplines. For instance, custom dressmaking is not necessarily your route to sure success, unless you are able to target an affluent customer base to which you provide select service and quality garments. It is possible to make a modest income with custom dressmaking, but you need to be vigilant about pricing and spending and be careful not to allow your customer to dictate your price point. There are always customers who will pay; sometimes you just have to search for them.

Compared to dressmaking, drapery and window treatments command a higher per-hour fee. There's a perception that sewn clothing should be cheaper than ready-to-wear but that anything for the home should (and does) cost more.

Why is this? In the past, people sewed for economy, and many can still recall their grandmothers, mothers, aunts and neighbors sewing clothing for them as a money-saving measure. But custom-made draperies, available at most department stores, were fairly expensive. The cheaper alternative was to purchase factory-made curtains at discount stores. In recent years many finer retail stores have closed these departments, and now the customer must have window treatments made in drapery workrooms or purchase them from decorators (who have them made in drapery workrooms). The result is that draperies and top treatments are now even pricier than they once were. In addition, newer homes with volume space and high windows have rendered the once "standard" window sizing useless. Nearly every window in the average new home is custom sized, making nearly every window treatment custom sized also.

Because of customer perceptions and the fact that there are fewer sources for specially made draperies, it's possible to gross three to six times as much per hour to sew custom window treatments as it is to make custom clothing. Also, the skill level is different; creating well-fitting clothing for the human form is among the most complicated of tasks. Window treatments utilize nearly all straight seams, thereby making them simpler to sew.

When you are known for doing one thing well, you receive better public awareness of your business. Word-of-mouth advertising is the cheapest but most effective of all ways to let the public know about your business. If your customers tell one another and potential new customers about your terrific way with a round window, or a bridal train, or altering a jacket sleeve vent, you are miles ahead of the game.

When you specialize, you eventually streamline your focus and, consequently, all your operations. You don't waste energy refocusing several times a day; you know what you're going to do each day, and each task becomes routine. Also, when you have a tough problem, it is more likely to be a repeat of a problem; eventually, less time is wasted in problem solving. This makes you more efficient and ultimately brings you more money per hour. It even streamlines your supply closet: If you only need tailoring interfacing, you won't waste the time or the money to purchase, or the space to store, bridal interfacing, for instance. If you're a bridal designer, you can concentrate your thread and lining investment in colors of white, off-white and ivory.

If you're known as a specialist, you will experience a faster track to success. Only those people who want your specific service will come to you, and you can focus on honing your craft in that one area. You may even consider centering your energy on two or three specialties as this can help even out seasonal swings in income.

By honing in on one or two markets, you can create more income for yourself also. When you have that market in focus, it enables you to pinpoint the marketing ideas that will work best. You won't waste time, and money, trying to sell air conditioners to Alaskans!

Here's a suggestion for defining your services for your customers: Practice presenting a thirty-second synopsis of your business that defines exactly what you want to be known for. For instance, if you are a childrenswear manufacturer, say so. Don't just say, "I make children's clothing." That's an invitation to the customer to take advantage of you and call upon you to do other sewing jobs. This wastes your time and energy and antagonizes prospective customers. Don't allow this to happen; describe your business specifically and in easy-to-understand terminology.

The worst thing you can say is, "I sew." That opens you up to any and all who want sewing done for them. Be specific, and help your potential customer make you successful.

# How to choose your niche

### Evaluate your skill level

Be brutally honest with yourself. Determine whether you have the fine skills to be successful. Are you truly ready to bill yourself as a couturier? Would you be intimidated working with interior designers with the slipcover-making skills you have now? Are you confident your production work is up to snuff? Would you pay the prices you'll set for the items you make for craft shows? In what skills do you excel?

### Evaluate your tolerance for people

Are you a people person, or would you rather work alone and just sew things? If you hate working with the public, choose a specialty that doesn't require direct contact with customers. Some crafts, production sewing, and some manufacturing, for instance, are specialties that can offer such seclusion.

### Pinpoint your own areas of interest

Can you dedicate yourself to making crib quilts for five years, or would you rather create lovely heirloom christening gowns? If you can sustain

# Chris Wilson

**Mystiques**
**Harker Heights, Texas**

Unable to find G-string lingerie in department stores, Chris Wilson began making it for her own personal use, then for a non-sewing friend. Although neither are strippers, her friend said Chris should sell to local clubs. Chris resisted the idea for awhile, but when she was laid off her job, she decided to try to make a business out of making dance costumes.

Harker Heights is situated about sixty miles from Austin, but it boasts the largest Army military base in the world. Nearby Fort Hood brings lots of young men to the area, and topless dance clubs abound. Chris started knocking on the doors of clubs to see if the dancers would be interested in buying her garments.

Chris and her husband, Jimmy, who acts as her bodyguard, usually began their "workday" at 7:30 P.M. They made the rounds of about four clubs, once or twice a week, selling a variety of clothing to the dancers, usually getting home shortly after closing time at 2:00 A.M. In the beginning, Chris says she only visited clubs that didn't charge her for admittance, but the better clubs charged her about 10 percent of her total sales for access to the girls' dressing rooms each evening. Now Chris makes the clothing for just one club, which has about 140 dancers.

"There's a lot of competition," says Chris. "There are four or five other people making costumes around here, so I have to be sure my things are different from theirs.

To keep up, I was making, then ordering, more elaborate pieces for awhile, but it didn't pay to do that, so I'm not anymore. Now I do more basic pieces: T-backs (thongs), hot pants, tube skirts (cut to a *V* in front), triangle tops and pareaus (wrap skirts)." Most of the garments Chris makes are made of Lycra fabric in prints and solids, and the dancers can request fancier treatments, or fabrics such as Lycra foils, for a glittery look under the lights.

"My prices are lower than some," she points out, "mostly because I stay with the basic styles. For a T-back, for instance, I charge about $25, but to add rhinestones, I double the price. Underwire tops with rhinestones go for about $200." Chris herself can make about $700 a night in sales, mostly to regular customers. Occasionally, a big tipper adds to her profit margin.

Chris also makes a $20 basic dress that she can't keep in stock—most places charge $40 for the same thing—and a longer gown of the same pattern for $100. The basic dress is made from Chris's own pattern and from inexpensive fabrics. This item takes her a mere fifteen minutes to make, using a home serger and a tabletop coverstitch hemmer.

When we talked, Chris was planning to buy industrial machines soon and to start a catalog service for clients outside her own community. She plans to start simply, doing all the sewing herself, then eventually to hire employees. A web page was already in the works at the time of our interview.

interest in your chosen field for twenty to fifty hours a week, you will be much more successful than if you force yourself to slave away in an area that doesn't appeal to you much. Go for the specialty you like best, as long as a market exists somewhere.

Determine whether you have superior knowledge in a particular specialty. As an example, people who ride and own horses have a wide variety of needs for sewn products, and each discipline has a different set of garments and accessories. Western saddle clothing differs greatly from hunter jumper gear. The various competitive riding areas sometimes require costumes for even the horses. If you or a family member rides and you have special insight into the kinds of merchandise preferred by the other riders in your circle, this could be your niche in the marketplace. The horse industry pumps over $3 billion into the U.S. economy per year. As a specialty, it offers rich possibilities.

### Determine your local market interests

Survey local interests before you invest anything in your business. If you buy a $3,000 sewing machine with the intent to embroider towels and baby items, you may be in for a rude shock to find that no one in your local area is interested in purchasing such services. Do your market research first, then make your decisions and purchases.

If you don't find a local market for your work, you may be tempted to respond to ads about doing piecework for money. Be careful about these companies. If the job hinges on you paying for kits, I advise against getting involved. There have been reports of earnest sewists working hard to comply with a company's supposed skill level only to have their work rejected. Legitimate offers will not require a monetary outlay on your part.

### Tap into a wider market

Would those same baby items sell at craft shows? Or could you offer your sewing services to a specialty group over the Internet? Kateri Ellison, a dressmaker in Washington, DC, has sewn for clients in other states. She requests that her clients send their measurements via E-mail. Patterns are made by computer so they can be easily adjusted. Garment designs are approved by mail, and the finished garments are sent via FedEx. She has had a wonderful response to this service from her satisfied customers, some of whom she has never met.

# Chris Llewellyn

Custom Sport
Bainbridge Island, Washington

With many years' experience in pattern drafting and designing for outerwear manufacturers in the Seattle area, Chris Llewellyn decided to use her knowledge to start her own business making sports outerwear. Because Chris and her family are all active in sports, this line of work comes naturally to her. Everyone skis, sails and rides. Each of them teaches at different ski schools, which brings them a lot of business. Students ask where she gets her pants and jackets, and they often end up buying some. She offers a group discount to some classes.

Chris and her two employees' sports outerwear includes ski school uniforms and other skiwear. One specialty is skiwear for children. One-piece suits for kids, hats and other outerwear articles fill one wall of Chris's light-filled second-story workroom. Custom Sport also makes uniforms for rowing teams across the country, cycling wear and lift operator clothing. Other products include riding school jackets, helmet covers with matching vests and saddle pads for riders, and more equestrian wear, mostly for cross-country jumping. Protective vests are required attire for jumping, and Custom Sport has created a niche in making them. "We have sold vests in every state but Alaska and Hawaii, so far," Chris says. "And since my son is going to school in Alaska, we will probably find some customers there, too." The vests require special equipment. Chris says visitors to her workroom are often surprised to see a bandsaw

and a drill press. Employees cut the thick foam with the saw and drill each piece with the press, for ventilation.

Custom Sport began its mail-order business in 1978. In addition to the various lines of activewear Chris offers, she also does patternmaking for other small manufacturers and is happy to work as a manufacturing facility, if her schedule permits. Between Chris and her two sewing employees, they make hundreds of technical outdoor jackets a year and ship orders all over the country.

Chris notes, "I love to see a guy walking into the shop who is 6'8". I know I can help him, because I know he has never had a good fit in outerwear." She goes on to explain, "I can make the sleeves long enough and can customize anything, depending on what the customer wants. They may see a Gore-Tex jacket they like, but prefer another color. I stock dozens of colors, so I can accommodate them. They might like an extra pocket on a sleeve; we can do that, too. A lot of people like bells and whistles in their coats. If they want to spend the money, well, we can manage it."

Chris uses only industrial machines, except an older Viking she keeps for buttonholes. "I don't know how you can make any money using a home machine," she says. "I don't think it's fair to charge a customer $35 an hour without using high-speed equipment—I can sew twice as fast using my industrial equipment. I have no problem with my machines, especially the computerized industrial. But if it ever has a problem I can just send the control panel out to the shop; the machine part can stay put." This is almost a requirement for Chris, as the closest shop is off the island. Other equipment at Custom Sport includes an old upholstery machine for making horse blankets, a computerized Juki with automatic backstitch and heel-operated presser lift and an industrial serger. All the catalog components are created on a Macintosh computer.

---

## Assess work space requirements

If you intend to make draperies, stage curtains, sails or awnings, be sure you have lots of room, with big cutting tables. Anything less will be impractical. However, some specialties don't require much room at all. Alterations, for instance, can be confined to a small space. You really only need room enough for about a 2' × 3' cutting area, a sewing machine, some kind of pressing station and perhaps a blindstitcher. Bridal alterations take more space, but perhaps you can set up a larger, temporary cutting area only when it's needed.

Teaching sewing takes up a lot of space, too—usually a whole room—unless you are teaching one-on-one classes or at another location, such as the local community center. You'll also need more equipment—sewing, cutting and pressing. However, if you have the space, the communication skills, the desire and ability to teach and a good potential student base, the financial rewards of teaching can be significant.

Some other ideas for you if you have a small apartment or little available work space: custom children's clothing, miniquilts, doll clothes, napkins and other household items, scarves and hats. This is by no means a complete list; the sky's the limit for ideas.

## Assess equipment needs

Although many start out in the sewing business using their home machines, this isn't necessarily the best idea (see chapter three). In a production business like Deborah Jackson's uniform service, industrial machines are an absolute requirement, for both speed and efficiency. Traditional tailoring requires the use of pressing equipment with more steam than the average household iron, and both an industrial gravity-feed iron and a vacuum board may be necessary for you to accomplish a professional-looking product. Your specialty and the size of your business will determine your equipment needs.

### Consider your personal abilities and limitations

Upholstering requires strength, as does sailmaking. The sheer effort of heaving furniture and heavy canvas around can sap limited strength. Are you exhausted by long hours of hand sewing? You may want to avoid making heavily beaded bridal gowns.

Are you good at math? Precise fit requires good arithmetic skills, not only in custom clothing, but in window treatments and slipcovers, as well as fittings for RVs, motorcycles, tents, banners and many other sewn products.

### Determine your accessibility to raw goods and maintenance resources

Running to the fabric store for a spool of neon orange thread at 2:00 A.M. isn't an option for most people, but there are sometimes problems that need to be resolved quickly. Most mail-order services can and will send orders out by next-day delivery service; it just might cost you more. You may also have to travel far to find equipment. Be sure to get as much maintenance information as possible, particularly if your business is in a rural or otherwise inaccessible area. If you live in the remote hinterlands of Wyoming or Maine, it may be difficult to find a good repair facility for your industrial machine. However, this sort of obstacle is easily overcome.

# Sometimes a specialty chooses you!

Is this situation familiar to you? You have been sewing for others for awhile and you suddenly realize that most of your time is concentrated in one or two specialties? You have acquired a reputation for creating beautiful wedding decorations, or well-fitting, high-quality suits, or the cutest children's room decorations anyone's ever seen. Well, go for it! If this is acceptable to you, back up and regroup. Change your marketing focus so it reflects this change in your business, and hone in on that area. Accentuate the positive.

# What kind of income can you expect?

This depends on several factors, geography, for instance. What is profitable in one area of the United States may not be in your area, and vice

# Traits for Success & Possible Income

| Specialty | Traits for Success | | Possible Gross Income Ranges |
|---|---|---|---|
| Dressmaking | Ability to sew quickly and accurately<br>Patternmaking skills<br>Fitting expertise<br>Diplomacy and tact<br>Self-confidence | Good taste<br>Knowledge of fashion and fabrics<br>Creativity<br>Excellent spatial ability | $2 to $40 per hour |
| Alterations | Same as dressmaking, plus:<br>Good to excellent sewing skills<br>Knowledge of how garments are made<br>Ability to judge fit | Communication skills<br>Problem-solving skills<br>Knowledge of proportion | $5 to $30 per hour |
| Custom Design | Same as above, plus:<br>Excellent patternmaking skills<br>Couture-level sewing skills<br>Advanced creativity | Exquisite taste<br>Knowledge of better fabrics<br>    and their use | $7 to $45 per hour |
| Bridal | Same as dressmaking, plus:<br>Excellent sewing skills<br>Alterations skills<br>Good design sense<br>Excellent hand-sewing skills<br>    (for beading) | Knowledge of recent trends<br>Patience and good<br>    communication skills<br>Ability to hold up under<br>    extreme pressure<br>Large work space, especially tables | $8 to $45 per hour |
| Tailoring | Same as custom design, plus:<br>Excellent tailoring skills,<br>    including pressing<br>Thorough knowledge of<br>    tailorable fabrics | Thorough knowledge<br>    of shaping techniques<br>Excellent customer service skills<br>Good understanding<br>    of body complexities | $8 to $50 per hour |
| Costumes | Good to excellent sewing skills<br>Patternmaking ability<br>Excellent fitting skills<br>Alterations skills<br>Ability to translate ideas into reality<br>For body puppets: engineering skills | Ability to create illusion that<br>    holds up to stage lighting<br>Dyeing and other fabric<br>    manipulation skills<br>Thorough knowledge of fabrics | $2 to $10 per hour (nontheatric)<br>$6 to $40+ per hour (theatric) |
| Home Decor | Good eye for color and fabric choices<br>Knowledge of home decor trends<br>Good to excellent sewing skills<br>Dressmaking skills, for certain details<br>Speed and pattern-matching abilities | Large work area<br>Industrial machines<br>Excellent math skills<br>Good communication skills | $6 to $40 per hour |

| Specialty | Traits for Success | | Possible Gross Income Ranges |
|---|---|---|---|
| Crafts | Creativity and originality<br>Tolerance for duplication of effort<br>Good selling/marketing skills<br>Good sewing skills | Knowledge of current trends<br>Willingness to travel to shows<br>Access to lower-priced raw goods | $0 to $40 per hour (depending on craft, market) |
| Embroidery | Willingness to work with computers<br>Desire to make many of one design | Good mechanical ability<br>Large work space for the machines | $10 to $70 per hour |
| Sport Goods | Excellent design skills<br>Knowledge of the sport<br>  and the customer<br>Knowledge of the marketplace<br>  and trends | Originality<br>Desire to make many of one design<br>Access to appropriate fabrics<br>Engineering ability<br>Good marketing skills | $6 to $35 per hour |
| Quilting | Excellent hand-sewing or machine skills<br>Knowledge of quilt patterns<br>Good eye for color and design<br>Good eye-hand coordination | Large work space<br>Excellent spatial ability<br>Strong eyes | $4 to $30 per hour (more for machine quilters) |
| Flags/Banners | Excellent spatial ability<br>Good eye for color and design<br>Good eye-hand coordination<br>Large work space<br>Desire to make many of one design | Factory sewing skills<br>Access to wholesale fabric sources<br>Knowledge of musical and religious<br>  information<br>Good selling/marketing skills | $6 to $35 per hour |
| Liturgical | Excellent sewing skills<br>Knowledge of religious symbolism | Access to fine fabrics<br>Patternmaking skills | $5 to $50 per hour |
| Teaching | Excellent communication skills<br>Empathy for beginners<br>Good understanding of the material<br>Pleasant, clear speaking voice | Access to large work space<br>  for hands-on classes<br>Sense of humor<br>Ability to inspire others | $6 to $40 per hour |
| Piecework | Ability to sew quickly and accurately<br>Tolerance for duplication of effort<br>Large work space<br>Willingness to work to a deadline | Industrial machines and access<br>  to repair facility<br>Proximity to industry that needs<br>  your services | $5 to $30 per hour |

versa. In some parts of the South, less is paid for dressmaking than in the North. On the other hand, heirloom sewing is valued much more highly in the South. In New York City, even though it's a big, cosmopolitan area, it may be more difficult to charge a higher amount for a custom suit than in a Midwestern city. Why? There are still many sweatshop situations in a big city, and labor is sometimes very cheap.

Many people in rural areas or small towns believe they can't charge as much as their big-city counterparts. This may or may not be true. If you have the only alterations business in the area, you can almost charge whatever you want. Your customers' only alternative may be to do the work themselves. It's just not true that "things are cheaper in the country." A gallon of milk, a loaf of bread, a tankful of gas, a haircut—these may actually cost more in rural areas.

There's only one surefire way to figure out what to charge: Do your market research. It's more labor intensive than the "guess-and-by-gosh" method, but it's the only way to attain a true picture of your earnings potential.

Skill level and personality also factor into income potential. See the chart below for more specific information, as well as an income range for each specialty.

# Hiring employees

If you decide to manufacture a product on a larger scale than a one-person operation, consult your local Internal Revenue Service office, as well as your accountant. Hiring employees creates more paperwork than working solo, but it may be worth the effort if you have a hot niche market you need to pursue.

Be wary of employing sewing subcontractors, those who sew for you in their own homes. There are federal restrictions on hiring contract sewing help for ladies garments, and the law changed substantially in 1994. The onus is on you, the business owner, to make sure those working for you also have other clients; if they work only for you, they are considered employees. In more than one case, this has caused serious problems for business owners who, during a seasonal lull in assigning work to their subcontractors, were notified that one or more of them filed for unemployment. Since the business wasn't paying for unemployment insurance for these people, it caused the authorities to scrutinize that business more carefully. Stiff penalties are levied against those who break this law, including high fines and seizure of all goods and fixtures.

Some states have restrictions that differ from the federal laws. Wisconsin, for instance, mandates an immediate $1,000 fine for *hiring* sewing contractors. To make sure you stay within the law, research both the local statutes and the federal requirements.

# CHAPTER 3

# Equipping Your Business

The first step in establishing any business is to equip yourself with the tools you need to get the job done. If you plan to make a living with your sewing, your sewing machine must be appropriate for the type and amount of work you'll be handling. There are three main classifications of sewing machines on the market today.

- *Domestic machines* are those used in the home. They are usually portable, (although some have tables), weigh very little and use household current.

- *Industrial machines*, those that are true industrials, typically have one function they perform extremely efficiently. They are not portable—in fact, some of them are enormous—and they have heavy-duty motors that normally have either oil pans or self-oiling systems. Many industrial machines are inappropriate for the typical home-based sewing business, but there are some smaller machines that are used frequently.

- *Commercial machines* are hybrids of industrial and domestic machines. They perform more than one function, usually both a straight stitch and a zigzag, and often have the capability of sewing in reverse (true industrial machines rarely sew in reverse for backstitching). Needles and feet may be interchangeable with domestic machine parts, and motors are normally smaller than the true industrials. However, these machines are not portable and require heavy-duty shop tables for their use.

# Choosing the correct machine for your workshop

One of the most appealing reasons to begin a sewing business is that you already have most of the equipment you need. However, for a long-term business, you might want to consider buying a stronger machine. Most domestic sewing machines carry warranties that guarantee their trouble-free use for as much as twenty-five years. This presumes the "normal" wear and tear that any typical household appliance might receive over the course of its useful life. In the case of a sewing machine, this means no more than twenty to thirty hours of use in a month. When that same machine is used in a business, the usage could soar to as much as eight hours a day, or nearly eight times as much as the same machine in even the most avid hobbyist's pursuit.

The generous warranties of domestic machines are not meant to cover such heavy wear. Therefore, most companies specifically exclude any kind of business usage in the wording of their warranties. Before you buy a machine, be sure to ask about any such clause; it could mean that if you burn up the motor of your expensive machine, you alone are responsible for replacing either the parts or the entire machine.

If you already have a machine you want to use, make a decision about how you will feel about any problems down the line. Are you prepared to simply buy a new machine if this one begins to show wear and tear? Or would you prefer to save that machine for certain tasks only, such as buttonholes or decorative stitching, and purchase a heavy-duty machine for utility stitching? Many alterations shops keep a home machine set up just to make buttonholes and use industrial and commercial machines for all other sewing. Some use relatively inexpensive home machines to make alterations and have a blindstitch machine for hems. The owners are prepared to replace their home machines when they wear out.

# Advantages of industrial/ commercial equipment

## Speed

With the average speed of a home sewing machine at between 700 and 900 stitches per minute (spm), a change to an industrial speed demon at 3,500 spm can mean a dramatic increase in productivity and efficiency. For long seams like those in draperies, bridal and special occasion gowns,

Industrial bar tack

and tents or awnings, these faster speeds can make a great deal of difference in your hourly income.

If your product is small, however, the speed may not make as big a difference in your overall efficiency. Doll clothes, for instance, are less efficiently made on an industrial machine, as are other small items. For such short seams, it would be overkill to use anything faster than a home serger. (Industrial sergers are as much as four times as fast as their domestic counterparts.)

## Power

In the quest for piercing power to sew such items as heavy-duty canvas or multiple layers of any fabric, you may want to look to industrial machines. Their heavier motors allow them to make the most difficult jobs easy. There are machines built for specific tasks—to sew leather, for instance.

Industrial and commercial machines are rated as to what kind of work they are best suited for, and this information, on "spec sheets" for each machine, is available from anyone who sells them.

## Maximum efficiency

If your needs require specialty machines, the sewing industry has them. For example, you may want to consider buying a buttonhole machine. These are not petite additions to your sewing room. Buttonhole machines are about the size of an undercounter refrigerator (though they sit on a table so you can operate the machine while standing). However, if you need the capability to sew thousands of the same-sized buttonholes, the purchase of such a machine can save you hundreds of hours and pay for itself many times over. Each buttonhole is made identically, based on a set size, in less than the time it would take to reset a typical home machine for each buttonhole. You can literally make hundreds of buttonholes in an hour. In addition, there may be an opportunity to rent the services of the machine to other sewing professionals in your area. Conversely, some tailor shops have buttonhole machines you can rent, or you can pay them per buttonhole for special projects or garments.

Other machines offer specific task completion, such as coverstitch machines, to seam and decoratively finish stretch seams; blindstitch machines, to make professional-quality hems; button-sew machines, to sew on buttons at blinding speeds. Double-needle machines are especially useful to create perfectly parallel rows of stitching, such as those used on hems for knit clothing.

There are even computerized industrial machines that allow you to preset the stitch length for specific tasks. For instance, production specialist Deborah Jackson can, with the help of her Hisico computerized industrial machine, sew hundreds of pockets onto hundreds of pants. She presets the machine to lock the beginning stitches, sew a predetermined number of stitches for the seam, then lock the stitch again, cut the thread and suck the thread end down beneath the machine into a waste receptacle. Now that's efficiency!

In addition to specialty machines, feet for hundreds of specific tasks are available to make your life more efficient and your work speedier. Piping,

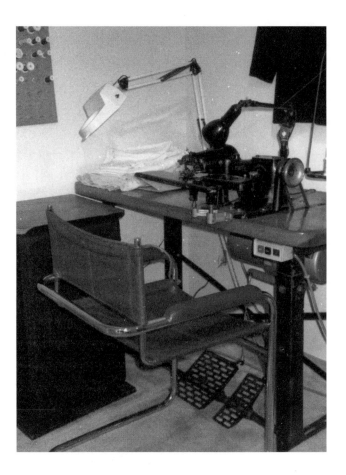

Industrial blindstitch machine

cording, folding and zipper feet are just a few of the ones available. How would you like to sew on miles of bias binding without ever lifting the presser foot and have none of it curl or twist? It's possible with the aid of folders that attach to the front of the machine to guide the bias onto the fabric perfectly. Hemming is another process made easier by specialty feet and folders. Hemmers are available in many widths for all sorts of applications.

## Duty use and maintenance

Because industrial machines are meant for factory use, they are also meant to run nearly continuously, often around the clock. This duty use, as it is known, makes for a virtually indestructible machine. Many models have self-oiling wicks, which keep the all-metal parts from heating too much and allow them to run without frequent maintenance interruptions.

Industrial buttonsew machine

---

On the other hand, the newer home machines have enclosed systems, using little or no outside lubrication. Although many of their parts are made of nylon or plastics, they are generally of a type that withstands the friction of "normal," or home, use. When they are used more frequently, these materials break down more readily, in particular the more sensitive computer parts of many electronic machines.

Although it's possible to maintain your own machines, it is generally better to have a qualified mechanic service them for you, especially for the more technical problems such as timing. Since industrial machines are less likely to break down for overuse and overheating but more likely to break down for timing problems, having a trustworthy mechanic nearby can be important. Machine stores generally have mechanics on staff or on call. Ask about this service when you purchase your machine.

# Buying a used machine

Although nothing lasts forever, most industrial machines can live almost forever. If you want to investigate using a factory model, consider buying a used machine; often they are in excellent condition and present a great value to the sewing professional. Such a buy could save as much as 60 percent of the original cost.

The chief disadvantage may be that the previous owner had the machine set to do tasks that aren't important to you. If you are buying directly from the owner, ask if she had the machine modified in any way to suit her work. Sometimes this will be a good thing, for example, if she had the motor speed set slower or faster than average and the new setting fits your needs. It could be important if she had specialty feet or attachments built, as parts aren't available at your corner fabric store. When considering buying a used machine, ask if you can also purchase the needles and bobbins that go with it. Having extras of each is a great time-saver.

Another disadvantage would be if the machine has not been properly maintained. Most factory machines are maintained by staff mechanics. However, smaller businesses may not take the time, money or energy to make sure their machines are running well. It's a good idea to check this.

# Space requirements

Industrial machines are usually much larger than their domestic counterparts. If your workroom is small, be prepared to give a large chunk of it to your industrial helpers. They are generally heavy, and definitely not portable, so plan ahead. Design a layout of the room, and keep your machines in that configuration for awhile (see "Space Needs for a Sewing Workroom," chapter four).

Along with being big and clunky, these machines aren't dainty and pretty like domestic models. The factory decor look will probably never hit the pages of *Architectural Digest*. Function is the key here. The all-metal, one-piece casings on the machine make it heavy enough to need a special table. These tables are made of heavy-duty Formica (you get your pick of green or woodgrain tops) and have steel adjustable-height legs. The motor mounts beneath the table, and the foot pedal is straddled between the

Industrial straight stitch machine

table's legs. To the right, also beneath the table, is usually the knee lift for the presser foot, a wonderful convenience for speed and control.

Most tables include a drawer or two for parts, as well as an extrawide top for supporting the fabric. If you find your product needs a larger table, a "corral" can be built to keep the fabric or garment off the floor.

# Pressing equipment

After sewing, pressing is probably the next most important process in a workroom. The need for heavy-duty equipment for this process is just as great, and in some cases, it's essential.

Heavy irons with gravity-feed water bottles for steam can make an enormous difference in the quality of your work and in the amount of time spent achieving that quality. In addition, a vacuum board is helpful

29

# Kim Lawrence

Kim's Custom Creations
Lanexa, Virginia

Six years ago Kim Lawrence wanted to work part-time. She had small children and needed a little extra income. A custom-decorating shop owner who had worked at Colonial Williamsburg hired Kim for awhile and taught her how to make window treatments and other items. When the owner decided to go back to Williamsburg to work and closed the shop, Kim continued the business from her home.

"I made up flyers advertising my new business, and my children and I placed them in newspaper boxes in the three secured neighborhoods in Williamsburg. I averaged one call for every 100 flyers we put out," Kim says. She spent about $20 for 500 flyers. At this rate, her cost per customer was about $4. And although these first few jobs were small jobs, they led to better assignments. Kim also ran twice-a-week ads in the Williamsburg community paper for $45 a month.

She originally worked with a home machine, right on the kitchen table. Kim recently bought both an industrial lockstitch and a blindstitch machine and is converting the garage to a sewing studio. Now Kim makes window treatments and other home accessories. She says, "I can sew anything for the home, including slipcovers, except upholstery. I make dust ruffles but send bedspreads out to be made by Virginia Quilting, about an hour away." Kim has done upholstery work, but admits "I'm not facile in it, and I don't quite know how to

charge at this point."

Kim's initial goal was to make $10 an hour. Some jobs bring in more than others. On one commercial rush job, she figures she made about $50 an hour, a rare event. This was for her best commercial client, who likes the quality of her work so he feeds her business. He often requests rush jobs, but he is positioning Kim to work for him more. "This was a $2,500 job that needed to be done in ten days. The fabric didn't come in for four of those days, so I only spent about six days sewing." Kim adds, "I would love to have more like that. There is lots of expensive commercial space in this area. For instance, I made three pairs of sheers for one building. I prefer the commercial jobs because I talk too much, and Mrs. Smith talks too much, and I end up not making any money on the time I spend with her."

Trial and error determined Kim's pricing. She got pricing information from bigger workrooms, and for jobs she didn't make any money on, she made sure she charged more the next time. According to Kim, "If people paid the price, I went up $10 next time. I got to a certain point where people wouldn't go for the price, so I kind of stuck there. There's a lot of major competition in my area, lots of top-of-the-line furniture stores." Kim adds, "To this day I can't say how long anything takes because I hardly ever get a chance to sit and finish something beginning to end."

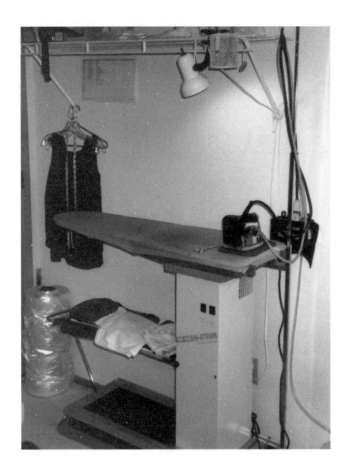

Vacuum board and industrial steam iron

in tailoring. It's an open secret that removing the steam from the fabric quickly and completely is key to creating a perfect press.

Just as it shares the unattractiveness and ungainliness of the industrial sewing machines, industrial pressing equipment also shares the efficiency of that equipment. It's also more expensive than the iron you can buy in any discount store, but well worth the extra expense and effort. Household irons are not meant to stay on all day, but the industrial versions' heating elements are well insulated from burning out. Their excellent steam is ready whenever you are.

# Finding sources

Larger cities have stores that sell industrial equipment, as do any smaller cities that have had any kind of textile industry in recent years. Companies that supply dry cleaners and tailor shops are also good sources for machines and other necessary supplies (see the appendix for specific sources).

To find a reliable local shop, ask other sewing professionals where they buy supplies. Your local dry cleaner may have information about a shop, as will any department store that has an in-house alterations department. This is also a great way to find maintenance specialists.

CHAPTER 4
# Setting Up Shop

Should your business be in your home or in a separate shop? Most sewing specialties work well as home-based enterprises. If you have the space, and the inclination, working at home is often the best way to begin. Naturally, if you decide to make massive stuffed costumes or theatre curtains and you live in a small apartment, home is probably not the optimal work space. However, if that is the specialty you've chosen, stick with it. Anything is possible—Deborah Jackson (see chapter one) has a factory in what was once her family room.

# Home-based business vs. a shop

There are many factors to consider when deciding whether or not to strike out to the "street," as an outside shop is often called. First of all, can you afford to pay rent? Can you afford not to? If your customer base is dependent on a visible presence in the community or on foot traffic past the shop, then a shop would be advisable. But when you're just starting out, it might be best to wait awhile to take this step. Here's an example of someone who has experienced both ends of this situation.

Gay Costa's alterations business began simply. She had worked in alterations at a department store that eventually went out of business. Gay found other retail store business, which she began doing from her home. When business increased, she remodeled her single-car garage to accommodate a couple of sewing machines, pressing equipment, a small fitting area and a customer area with phone and desk. Her daughter and her mother helped out with the business as needed.

Within a few months, Gay realized the garage wasn't going to provide enough space for her quickly growing business, and when a storefront near her home went up for lease, she contracted for the space. The best part about the location was its position directly in front of the drive-in window of the only bank in her small town. It wasn't long before everyone in the village of Greenhills, Ohio, knew of Galina Alterations' existence!

# Becky Reeves

Reeves Manufacturing/Xander Wear
LaSalle, Colorado

Reeves Manufacturing sews a variety of products, but the company started with sportswear for bodybuilders, which is still its main product.

In the summer of 1992, Becky Reeves opened Xander Wear, a shop in the small farming community of LaSalle, Colorado. The shop specializes in attire for bodybuilders, who have difficulty finding clothing that fits, as their necks and upper torso are generally much thicker than the average consumer's. Xander provides workout wear, some street clothing, bike shorts, baggies and big tops for kids. Becky makes all items in the line.

Originally, Becky worked from the basement in her home, and she worked at the business part-time. However, she soon outgrew the basement and took over the garage. She has been working full-time for the past couple of years, since her youngest child went to school.

Becky now has an 800-square-foot workroom attached to Xander Wear's store. This has worked out well; since customers must enter her shop through the store, they can only see Becky during store hours unless they have scheduled appointments, a boon for this mother of three school-age children. Also, Becky feels safe working alone, and if she has to leave for an hour or so, as she does at the end of every school day, the Xander personnel can take messages from walk-in customers or direct them to wait for her return. Becky says there are pros and cons about working in a storefront business, but her arrangement has many benefits.

"I have a section for sewing, a section for cutting, plus an office space. It's nice to have all the machines out of my home," she says. Becky has eight industrial machines, including a walking foot, a tailor's machine, a zigzag machine, a waistbander (for sewing several rows of stitches at once), a serger, a coverstitch machine and a blindstitch machine. In addition, she has a cutter with an 8-inch blade and chain mail gloves for safety.

Terry Reeves does all the cutting, although this isn't his full-time job. He and Becky have decided he will keep his "day job" as an electrician while the children are in parochial school, mainly for the benefits. Becky says the income from the business has doubled every year, but it still isn't enough to totally support them and provide tuition for three kids. Eventually, though, they would like to work together full-time, as well as hire employees to share the workload.

Becky's advice to anyone interested in her kind of business: "Make sure you love it. You will invest both time and money in the business; make sure you want to do both."

Gay Costa's corner workstation

Gay Costa's reception area

Business boomed, and Gay hired employees to help with the work, as by now her daughter had married and moved away. Several years later, Gay's daughter moved back to town with a new baby and decided to work with her mother again. They closed the store and moved back to the garage so they could keep the baby with them, and since Gay by now had a loyal customer base, they no longer needed the visibility of the storefront.

# Advantages of a home-based business

## Lower initial and operating costs

A commitment to a lease or expensive retail space could sink a new business before it really has a chance to get off the ground. With a home-based business, you can test the waters for awhile and see if your idea has merit. You can find out if your perceived market is really there, and you don't have to spend much more than the cost of a few hundred business cards to do so. In a home-based business, you can use the equipment you already have, including your existing phone line (see chapter nine). Any retail space would need a business phone (with a yellow pages listing), business utilities, rent, additional employee costs, more advertising money and other hefty expenses.

## Easier transition to starting a business

Home-based operations allow you to ease into business. Unless you know you have a solid market ready to beat a path to your door immediately, there may be some lag times at first. Many people start sewing for others part-time while working at other jobs until the sewing business begins to create a substantial replacement income.

## Less financial, physical and emotional commitment

Having a retail storefront costs a great deal initially, plus there are ongoing expenses, the largest of which is likely the rent. It's unusual to find monthly leases for retail spaces except in low-stability areas, so one- to three-year leases are more common—which may be a long time for a sewing business.

Operating a retail outlet also requires a tremendous amount of your physical and emotional energy. Someone needs to be at the store for all the stated hours, and someone has to be able to handle every need of the business. At first, this is usually the owner, unless ample start-up business or capital allows for employees to do these chores. This would only be possible in rare situations, though, and generally the owner is on the line for such time-consuming jobs. A big emotional drain is the constant worry over whether enough money will come in to cover operational costs, many of which would not exist for a business conducted from home.

## Close proximity to family members

Home-based businesses offer a way for many people to "have it all": to provide an additional income to the family while still maintaining a presence in the home. If you need to stay home with children or an older family member, a home-based business can be very helpful. In fact, one study suggests that a second wage earner working outside the home in the U.S. actually costs the family money, because of expenses such as car fare, child care, work-related clothing and meals eaten away from home.

While Becky Reeves's factory is outside her home, she still closes her shop to drive her children home from school every afternoon. Many store situations would not lend themselves to such a setup, however.

Your own health problems or unusual schedule requirements may also make it more desirable to work from home. You can work whenever it's convenient to you. If you're the type who doesn't really come alive until the kids are in bed, being able to sew quietly into the night can be a tremendous advantage over outside work. Kitty Stein's husband works the night shift, and she enjoys working when the house is quiet and there are no phone calls.

## Use of existing equipment and space

Buying equipment adds more financial burden to the start-up of your business, as does adding on to a house or renting another space. Keeping your current setup of machinery and space will work for awhile (unless the specialty has additional needs), and you can always expand later.

# Disadvantages of a home-based business

## Possible illegality

Although many communities have loosened their laws on home-operated businesses, it's wise to find out what the law says in your particular area. Some towns, especially planned communities, have stringent rules about what types of businesses are allowed and about how these businesses may be conducted. In order to comply, you might have to change your focus slightly, or even apply for change in the laws. Also, be careful to check what permits are required.

## Constant presence of your work

If you're the type who obsesses over unfinished projects or who can't seem to quit work, a pile of work awaiting you in the next room may be difficult to ignore. When phone calls come in or customers come to the studio, having a little space between your work life and your home life is often desirable. It can be achieved; it just may be difficult.

# Customer drop-ins and phone calls at odd hours

This doesn't have to happen. If you're clear with customers about your business hours, much of this problem won't exist. Having a second phone line and an answering machine or voice mail helps, too. Simply avoid answering calls to that line after hours, and include your business hours in your answering machine message. A direction to customers to call back during that time is helpful.

Judy Pagenkopf has an alterations shop in a separate area of a laundromat and a home-based alterations and custom dressmaking business. She tells her customers her hours and insists that outside of those hours they see her on an appointment basis only. "I'm busy after dinner," says this single mother of three. "I have a report on Australia to work on, posters for art and long division to figure out. My customers have to understand that my children need me in the evenings."

# Interference with your family life (and vice versa)

When deadlines loom, trips to your child's school for special occasions often take a backseat. That bride who loses fifteen pounds in the last month before her wedding may need her gown altered just as your seventeen-year-old child is choosing a college. A large order for backpacks for a hiking club may have to be set aside when a family member has a serious illness. Self-employment means being prepared for these sorts of emergencies. A home business often causes collisions between the domestic and the business sides of your life.

If your business needs to function in a part of your house that was previously available to the rest of the family, that disruption of the rhythm of the home could mean discord for awhile. Usually, this doesn't last. As my own business grew and changed, it migrated through various parts of the house, from spare bedrooms, to half the basement, to the end of the living room, to the entire family room. My family adapted, although they grumbled a bit at first.

Sometimes family members who are unhappy about the business purposely get in your way. Preparing the whole family in advance, and enlisting their cooperation, may forestall such a problem.

## Inability of your home to support the business

Do you have enough room for the business you want? Or, if you have the room, is it comfortable enough? Most homes aren't equipped with enough overhead lighting to accommodate the high lighting needs of sewing and pressing. You may find it's difficult to safely plug in enough lighting and sewing appliances in the space you have. A boost in the home's electrical capacity might also be in order. The same cool basement studio that was comfortable for a class of six sewing students was too chilly for my own office, which had to be moved elsewhere.

How about an attractive area to greet customers? For dressmaking and alterations, a private area for trying on garments is the bare minimum of publicly accessible space you need. Do you really want customers going to your bedroom area to change in the only bathroom? Is it possible to create a private spot for this purpose with a screen or some other method? Would you feel better if customers could enter the work area directly, without access to the rest of your home? If you decide to teach sewing, is there a convenient place for students to try on their garments?

Some specialties may have tremendous storage or other physical needs. For instance, an embroidery business that requires storage of hundreds of spools of thread, two computers and five large embroidery machines may not be welcome in the typical home. Neither will the traffic of customers coming in and out, if your family is used to having more privacy.

# Space needs for a sewing workroom

Often, a business gets started before the owner realizes what is happening, or it grows so quickly that space is soon cramped. In a situation like this, little initial thought goes into planning the workroom. And if employees are added to the space, everything may soon change from varying degrees of efficiency to total chaos.

If you find yourself in one of these scenarios, it is probably time to consider rearranging things.

- Do you have trouble finding things immediately?
- Are you constantly maneuvering around furniture to get from one task to another?
- Must any tasks be completed in another room or on another floor because space is so limited?
- In order to cut out projects, is it necessary to clear off a space? (Or do you find yourself crawling around on the floor to hem draperies or tents?)
- Is the clutter beginning to bother you?
- Have you ruined anything lately because of clutter?
- Have you found yourself buying duplicates of notions you already own?

Planning a work area takes a little effort, but in the long run it saves time. A well-thought-out workroom design can make an enormous difference in your efficiency, no matter how much or how little space you have available.

# Beginning to plan your work space

First examine the space; take stock of its physical features. Are there windows (or a lack thereof) that offer wonderful light part of the day? Do those windows let in too much glare or the heat of the day? Would a different covering make a difference? Do the dark walls feel oppressive?

How about the rest of the lighting? Is it sufficient to keep your eyes from fatiguing, or would more light help you work longer? (Tip: Almost no room has *too* much light!) Are dark walls or furnishings absorbing what light there is? Do the fixtures have sufficient wattage to illuminate the area? Note any areas you feel need more light.

What about your work flow? Would it be better to have a cutting area set up nearer to the sewing machines, or would you prefer to have a pressing station closer to the machines? What tasks require you to get up from the chair most often every day? Would it help if you could sit down for them, or would a shorter walk make it easier for you to accomplish these tasks? Think of the different things you do in a typical workday; how would you improve the flow of such a day?

Storage is everyone's problem. As amateurs twenty years ago, we didn't need much more than a machine and a sewing basket to accomplish all kinds of wondrous things. Today's professional workroom boasts many labor- and timesaving devices and requires storage space for a long list of supplies: interfacings, trims, threads, machine supplies, bolts of fabric and completed projects. Organization is crucial to efficiency and profitability. List all the items you need to store and where they need to live in relationship to the rest of the workroom; for example, all the press cloths, tailor hams, clappers, etc., need to be near the pressing area.

*Ergonomics* is a buzzword today that means adapting the working environment to the needs of the human body. Better chairs, higher cutting tables and more comfortable tools all help make your workday more pleasant. What are your particular difficulties in the present space? Is your current chair uncomfortable after an hour or so of sewing? Does your back scream with pain after a cutting session? Are the scissors you use giving you blisters? Look for ways to make your work more comfortable. And don't forget to take breaks! Sitting too long is hard on the body; changing position every forty-five minutes to an hour is beneficial, and reduces eyestrain as well.

List various space needs of your particular business.

- Sewing—can be divided into various sections, such as seaming, hemming, embroidery, serging, buttonholes, buttons, topstitching
- Pressing
- Cutting
- Customer reception/consultation
- Fitting
- Paperwork/telephone/messages
- Computer/office
- Storage—for customers' goods
- Customer and/or employee restroom
- Shipping/packaging

# Measuring the work space

The next step is to measure the room(s). This isn't difficult, but it needs to be accurate. Begin at a corner. Measure along each wall, writing each measurement as you take it. In a rough drawing, indicate each door and

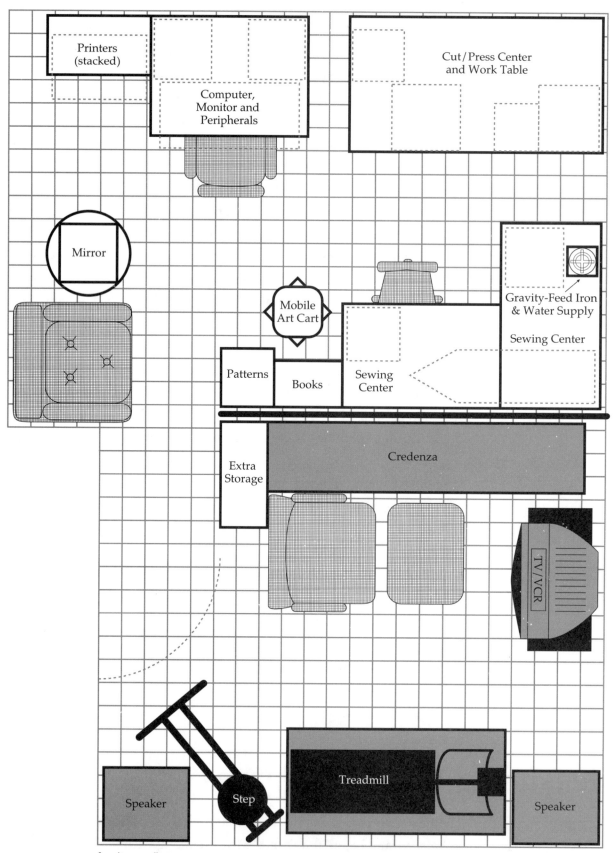

**Sample space diagram** (One grid square = 6")

window opening and their positions along the wall, as well as wall outlets, lights and switches. Measure from the floor to the bottoms of these features, also, so you can tell how much room is beneath each one. Using a good metal rule like the ones carpenters use, measure to the nearest ¼ inch.

Plot this on graph paper, using ¼-inch grid, with a scale of one square equaling six inches. Since most rooms are not perfectly square, don't be too concerned if your measurements aren't exactly right, unless your home or building is fairly new or the dimensions are off by more than a couple of inches. A good scale ruler can help with drawing the room. Triangular rulers are probably the most common, available at an office or art store in the drafting department. Draw a circle on the plan to indicate each overhead light so you are sure to take them into consideration. Note any architectural features you need to work around, such as poles and heaters. Also indicate closet areas and dimensions.

Now that you have the room drawn, you can begin to plot a space diagram. Make several photocopies of this graph so you can write on them and discard them without redrawing the measurements. Now you are ready to design a plan. Since paper is easier to move than actual furniture, especially if the furniture is in another room or on another floor, make scale drawings of everything that will go in the room, and cut them out to use as templates. (Tip: If you cut these from different colored paper, they will be easier to see against the graph paper.)

Note: You may prefer to use one of the many CAD-based drawing systems for designing your plan. Input the measurements of the room, and create your own furniture pieces from the library included in the program. (Many programs allow you to edit the dimensions of the icons in the library.) Using such a program will allow you to save many versions of the plan, and you can also "see" the plan in the program's 3-D view.

Considering the different areas you need for your business, begin to look critically at the actual area. How can you place each center for maximum efficiency? For instance, ask yourself whether it might be best to keep customers out of the sewing area, which may be messy. If the answer is yes, decide how to locate customer reception elsewhere. If your work is particularly neat, or if you haven't any additional space, you may decide that your customers can just as easily be greeted in the workroom. Some specialties, production sewing or many craft-type businesses don't require this type of area. Do you require easy access to a washing machine? Factor that into your plans as well.

On one of your photocopied room diagrams (I'll call this Plan One), draw circles where you would like to locate various work centers. For instance, if there is a wonderful window you'd like to take advantage of, place a sewing area circle there. Nearby should be pressing and storage and any other work processes that pertain to your business.

Next, consider how you need to work. Is it really efficient to have the cutting table across the room from the sewing area? It is if you do all your cutting first and then sew. For some quilters or wearables artists, that wouldn't be practical. In order to add color and pattern as the creative urge strikes, they may need a cutting area adjacent to the sewing machine.

When thinking about your work flow, consider the work triangle. For most sewing processes, the three "legs" of the triangle would be cutting, sewing and pressing. Production sewing is usually done on precut fabric and is rarely pressed by the manufacturer, so only the sewing area is needed. However, a place to receive the cut goods and to prepare them for shipping or pickup may be equally necessary. In addition, somewhere to lay out the various pieces in order of sewing is desirable.

Note: If you have employees, the ideal setup gives each person, or group of persons, a work triangle that won't be intersected by someone else.

# Various layouts

Basic layouts for the ideal work triangle include L-shaped, U-shaped, one-wall and corridor. These options offer varying degrees of efficiency, and your choice will depend on the room's physical features and your personal preferences.

## L-shaped and U-shaped layouts

These are the most efficient of all setups for a sewing workroom. Every-thing is easily accessible, particularly if the operator is using an office-type swivel chair with wheels. A mere twist of the hips will propel the operator from the sewing machine to the pressing station. This is an ideal setup for anyone who needs to work quickly at multiple tasks, for instance, making doll clothing or other small items. The operator could cut out the

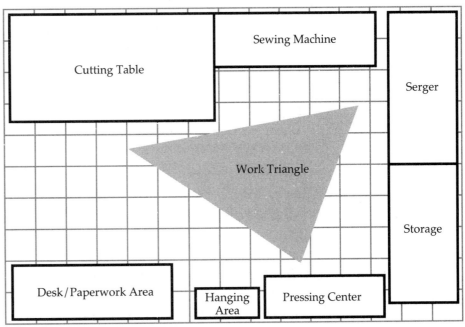

**U-Shaped Layout** (One grid square = one foot)

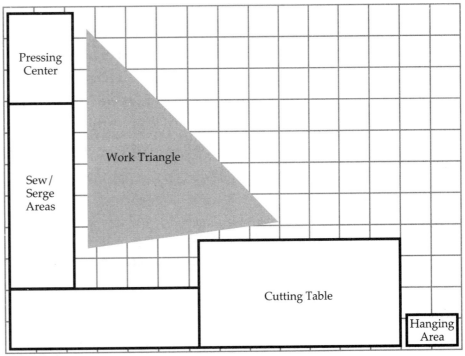

**L-Shaped Layout** (One grid square = one foot)

pattern, then go immediately to the machines to sew the garments. Pressing requires only another movement, particularly if the ironing board or pressing board is set at chair height.

The main reason these layouts work best is because they keep traffic

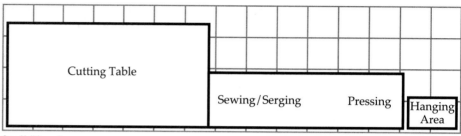

**One-Wall Layout** (One grid square = one foot)

out of the main work area; traffic tends to flow around the L or the U rather than through it.

## One-wall and corridor layouts

Since traffic can flow past or through this type of arrangement, plan carefully so tasks aren't subject to constant interruptions. Also, unless a chair with well-lubricated casters is used, the operator must physically get up and move to various stations to perform other tasks. Sometimes all you can find is one wall, though, so it's better than nothing.

Even with only one wall, an L-shaped or U-shaped layout can be created using various furniture arrangements. Cutting tables and pressing stations that can be moved to the operator's side can create either of the more efficient arrangements temporarily. For small areas or where nothing can sit out except work in progress, this is an ideal solution.

# Storage

Everyone struggles to create efficient and sufficient storage, in any kind of business. But sewing especially creates storage problems because of the many kinds of notions and patterns used every day.

What kind of workroom do you envision as the ultimate work space? Does it have everything at your fingertips, displayed in the open? Or do you prefer to have the neat, clean look of closed storage, with everything behind doors or in drawers? Most people will end up with some combination of the two preferences.

Identify your storage needs. List the things you use frequently, and prioritize them in order of importance. On the photocopied plan you designed earlier, add a few more circles to indicate storage space. Using colored ink or pencil, define where you think various items should be kept for the highest efficiency. This will give you a better idea of how to organize the space.

# Open storage

If there are no closets, or if seeing all your supplies gives you a creative boost, open storage is ideal. Residing on shelving that reaches to the ceiling or on racks hanging from walls, fabric and supplies can lend their color and form to the decor of the room. Small items can be placed in colorful bins or other containers available at any of dozens of stores who cater to office and home storage needs. Open baskets are wonderful for holding quilt fabrics, and wire shelving actually allows air to flow around anything kept on them—perfect for fabric and other fragile supplies.

# Closed storage

Fabric and thread are both susceptible to damage from light, heat and dust. If this is a concern in your work space, then by all means consider keeping them protected from these factors. You may also prefer the uncluttered look of having everything stashed away. But what do you do if your space doesn't have walls and walls of closets?

Can you create storage under tables? Cutting tables afford a large space for storage. One designer has a lovely, light-filled workroom with absolutely no clutter. When asked where she kept everything, she swept aside the fabric draping the edges of her cutting area and other tables. Boxes, drawers and shelves were holding fabric, notions and other supplies. Velcro holds the draping to the tables' edges, allowing easy access to anything beneath the surfaces. The draping also contributes color and a designer touch to the decor and provides a bit of soundproofing as well.

Is a closet available for your use? If not, how about creating one? If there is an area of the room that can be enclosed, you can create wonderful closed storage simply by installing a floor-to-ceiling miniblind or cellular shade. Shelves and cubbies can be erected behind such a blind, which can also add decorative and perhaps sound-insulating value. A useful hiding place can even be created with a simple folding screen.

Kitchen cabinets can be modified for use in a sewing room. They don't necessarily have to become a permanent part of the room. If you only use base cabinets, many times they can be freestanding units, perfect as a base for cutting tables. Topped with some kind of sturdy surface, they are the perfect height for comfort while cutting, and they offer lots of storage possibilities. Research the many cabinet options available—pullout shelves can be utilized for machine storage; drawer dividers are great for grouping threads; extra-deep drawers, such as for pots and pans, offer great space for storing rolled-up interfacings, and these drawers can be opened all the way so with one glance you can see everything inside. Use your imagination; you may surprise yourself.

# Lighting

Now that you know where you will work and where everything is to be placed, plan how to adequately illuminate those areas.

Did you know that your eyes use about 25 percent of your body's energy? Even more endurance is called for during activities with high lighting requirements. Activities such as sewing, cutting, writing, reading and ironing, performed over sustained periods of time, can sap your energy under poor lighting conditions.

You may have already experienced fatigue during a workday and wondered why something as seemingly innocent as sewing would tire you out so. The solution could be as simple as adding more light to the room. The better the lighting in your workroom, the more quality time you'll spend there, and the more efficient you'll be.

# Wall color

Another problem affecting a room's lighting may be that the walls are too dark. One way to take advantage of the available light, even magnify it, is to paint all the reflective surfaces, such as walls and ceilings, a light color. Even on a bright day, a room with ample lighting and windows but dark walls will still seem dark. Walls painted a balanced white, between stark white and cream, potentially reflect as much as 80 percent of the ambient light back into the room. Compare this to dark walls, which may reflect as little as 10 percent of the available light. Be sure to use flat or semigloss paint, as high gloss can cause a glare that can actually reduce the effectiveness of the light-colored walls—and give you a nasty headache to boot.

# Natural light

Windows are natural light emitters, except on gloomy days or at night. And if the window is facing south, the resulting glare on sunny days can have a negative effect instead of enhancing the room's lighting.

Window coverings are almost as important as lighting. Use your window coverings to cure any insufficiency in the window. For instance, if there is a glare on some days, a cellular shade in a light color will soften the sunshine without reducing its light value, as well as insulate the room from the sun's heat. That same shade will help augment the room's lighting at night, too. Nighttime windows with no coverings can have the same effect as a dark wall; you will notice light actually being drawn away by the blackness of the uncovered window.

Don't forget office duties when planning lighting. Allow for some kind of direct illumination of the desk or other workstation.

# Kinds of lighting

## General lighting

- Grouped as two kinds: direct and indirect
- Includes ambient light, or room light—can come from windows, wall and ceiling colors or mirrored surfaces
- "Washes" a room with light

## Task lighting

- Used for close work—includes any direct light
- Pinpoints the light
- Illuminates the work without throwing shadows over it
- Helps avoid shine or glare in your eyes

On your Plan One diagram, which already includes circles indicating work centers and storage, draw additional circles with a highlighter to indicate where light is needed most. Determine where direct lighting should be located, for example, over the sewing machines (to augment any other light there), over cutting tables, near pressing stations. Don't forget that dressing and fitting rooms should also be well lit, with strong general lighting. The one rule to follow: Accept no shadows.

Now you're ready to implement Plan One. Lighting should be installed first. There are a variety of bulbs and fixtures available; your needs may be met best with a combination of light types.

## Incandescent bulbs

Today's incandescent bulbs are more versatile than ever before. With options ranging from cool white to full spectrum, most existing fixtures can be made to perform well in a workroom. Incandescent light, which tends to be more direct than fluorescent, is best for task lighting.

Look for clamp-on fixtures for industrial sewing machines. These are perfect for not only machine sewing, but for directing light on hand sewing and ironing as well.

Choose full-spectrum incandescent bulbs for better perception of color values when making color matches in fabric or craft materials. This can also be a health benefit if you suffer from Seasonal Affective Disorder (SAD). Full-spectrum bulbs mimic the color of real sunshine and are often recommended by doctors for anyone with this problem.

## Fluorescent fixtures

In addition to their energy-saving benefits, fluorescent bulbs offer a more even wash of light, and manufacturers have made major technological advances. Today's fluorescents offer the same range of choices as incandescents, including red-band, blue-band and full spectrum. Some even fit into lamps meant for traditional light bulbs. When augmented by incandescent or halogen task lighting, fluorescent fixtures are especially good for lighting large areas.

# Kateri Ellison

Designs by Kateri
Washington, DC

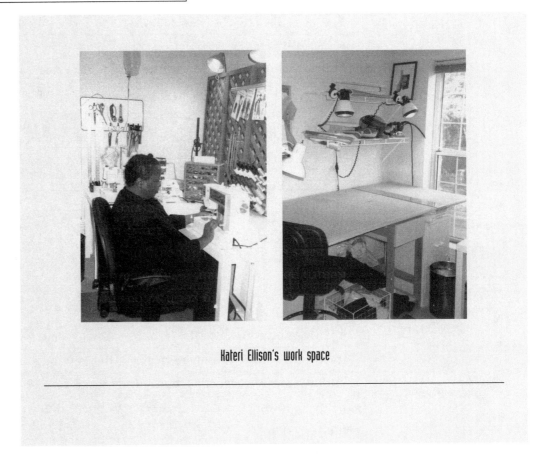

Kateri Ellison's work space

Because of limited space in her Washington, DC, townhouse, custom clothier Kateri Ellison designed her workroom/office for total efficiency.

In a space roughly 8½' × 14', Kateri has everything she needs to conduct business on a typical workday. Because she works alone, Kateri has taken advantage of the size of the room to make it work best for her. Without leaving her chair, she can sew, serge, press and answer the phone or fax. Ample electrical outlets supply power to the workroom and office equipment and lighting.

Two closets, one on each side of the room, offer clutter-free closed storage. Also,

Kateri uses the space beneath the work and cutting tables as storage. Filing cabinets and drawers store all kinds of sewing paraphernalia.

A comfy chair with a stack of current fashion magazines nearby makes a pleasant spot for customers to sit while planning their next wardrobes. An attractive wall divider affords the customer privacy during fittings, and it breaks the room into two parts so one portion is also available for the Ellison family's use. An Oriental carpet over the room's wall-to-wall carpet further divides the room visually.

One side of the divider makes an excellent backdrop for the bulletin board used as a project control center above the sewing machines. Pattern envelopes and swatches of customers' fabric pinned to the board allow Kateri to monitor work in progress. Above the wall over the cutting table, inspirational photos and draped fabric stimulate the creative juices and add an attractive accent to the room.

To augment the natural light that streams in from the two windows, generous track lighting illuminates the work areas. Mini-blinds disappear when open during daylight hours then reappear to preserve Kateri's privacy when she is sewing in the evening.

## Halogen bulbs

Relative newcomers to the lighting scene, halogen bulbs offer a wonderfully true color of light, perfect for the sewing room. Though they are initially more expensive than either incandescent or fluorescent bulbs, halogen is less expensive per hour to burn than incandescent, similar to fluorescents.

There is a drawback to using halogen lights: They are very hot; in fact, they are often used as wonderfully efficient heating elements in kitchen cooktops. This unfortunately makes them not only uncomfortable but also more dangerous to use. If you choose halogen for your workroom, make sure the bulbs and fixtures are labeled *UL approved*, and be extra careful to keep the lights away from curtains, walls and anything else flammable. The recommended distance is twelve inches or more. Also, choose fixtures that have guards over the bulbs to help protect fingers or other objects that might hover too close.

One particularly effective use of halogen bulbs is in torchère-type lamps aimed at the ceiling over a cutting table. With a white ceiling this efficiently illuminates a cutting area. And if you choose the type of torchère fixture that has a clear or frosted shade, the light also illuminates the rest of the room. One of the most effective of this type is the fixture with the light on a swing arm. This can be positioned nearer to the cutting area than the stationary standing light.

# Professional attitude and image

When customers come into your workroom or your shop, they will immediately form an opinion about you and about your work. Unless you will never have anyone come to your workplace, a clean, organized workroom can mean the difference between gaining your customer's respect and not getting it at all. Not every customer feels this way, but there will be some who will not work with you if they feel your studio is dirty and untidy. There will also be those clients who know that creativity comes from chaos—those people are to be cherished!

When you greet clients for the first time, you should make an effort to dress neatly and at least have the floor swept and the most serious clutter banished from sight. Instill confidence from the beginning. While it is normally not necessary to wear a suit and heels, contrast your own reaction to someone dressed neatly with a touch of makeup to that same person with uncombed hair, dressed in ragged sweatshirt, faded, baggy jeans and grubby tennies. Which person would you feel better about handing a project that could cost you hundreds of dollars? If the external clues of dress are all you have to go on, you would probably prefer the one who is better groomed.

Make sure the rest of your family conforms to the business attitude also. This doesn't mean your seven-year-old should wear a business suit, but it does mean that children don't compete with you for their share of clients' attention. Bridal expert Karen Howland's five children knew that when "the pretty ladies" came to be fitted for bridal gowns, the kids weren't to disturb their mother unless it was an emergency. A door between her studio and the rest of the house was shut during fittings, which emphasized the need for privacy, but Karen could still hear what was going on. When the youngest child was alone with her during a fitting, he was occupied with small toys kept just for that purpose.

Clients should not be greeted at the door by a sticky kid or on the telephone by, "Who is this?" If your business is home based, having both a separate entrance and a separate phone line that are only answered in a businesslike manner could be beneficial. If these are not possible, regular reminders to the family might be necessary for awhile until your priorities are remembered consistently. I'm speaking from personal experience here. My own family was forbidden to answer the line reserved for my sewing school. When I answered that line, it was with a cheery, "Hello, this is Karen," or, "Good morning, this is Karen." Voice mail on that line took care of answering machine messages gone astray due to overzealous little message erasers. ("It wasn't for me" or "I thought you heard that message!") Be sure your answering machine message also reflects a business attitude.

When phone calls come in and you're in the midst of taking care of another customer, it's common courtesy to wait on the person who was there first. Is there anything more infuriating than waiting for a salesperson in a department store as he answers the telephone? If you don't have an answering machine that can field calls, take a message and return the call when you aren't as busy. One excellent reason above and beyond customer service: Interruptions cause mistakes. Because of a phone call, I once cut an entire faux fur coat with half the grain going the wrong way.

About customer service: Ascribe to the idea that "a bird in the hand is worth two in the bush." Don't alienate the paying customer in front of you in your anxiety to get new business. You could end up losing both. Return phone calls right away, regardless of whether they involve potential sales or problems with current or previous projects.

Service problems tend to grow; nip them in the bud immediately. If there's a conflict between the service you feel you rendered the client and the service she perceives she has received, resolve it as soon as possible. Problem resolution is difficult for some people; if this is your own weak point, refer to your library for help. Many books have been written about sales, and many of them have chapters on this issue. This is also a common discussion topic of professional sewing and other networking groups.

# Keeping track of your work

As your workload increases, it will become more difficult to stay organized, unless you have a way to keep tabs of the status of each project. Patricia Anthony, of Wyldwmn Custom Clothing, uses a calendar as an organizational tool. She explains, "I have a project calendar on which I mark out all my 'personal' time and business appointments. Then as each client or project comes in, I schedule the hours right on the calendar. Unless I am expecting a specific, important call from a client, I am unavailable by phone during my production time." Patricia returns calls first thing in the morning or between 7:00 and 8:00 P.M. when people are home from work.

To fill in blank space on your calendar, Patricia advises, "What you can do is schedule in your own personal projects . . . the clients don't know that they are your private projects. That way if you need to reschedule them, you can do that easily by telling your client that you know that the deadline on that project is far enough off that you can easily reschedule it. It gives your calendar a successful look right from the beginning."

Patricia also offers her customers "overtime" hours at premium rates. She says, "I do limit the number of overtime hours each week so as not to lessen the quality of work I do on other projects. I make it a point to explain this to my clients so that they don't go away thinking that at some time someone else's emergency may impact the quality of time I spend on their garments or my ability to meet one of their deadlines." Patricia goes on to say, "I *never* suggest that I might 'put off' someone else's work, because then that client may think I will do the same to them at some point and then rush through their project."

Another suggestion for staying on top of all projects: Attach an input slip to all parts of a project as soon as it comes in. Keep that slip with all other paperwork related to the project—work orders, time records, order changes, receipts for any supplies pertaining to this job—until the customer picks up the finished work. A plastic zip-top bag is a good receptacle for these items: Enclose smaller projects in the bags with the paperwork, and for garments, punch holes in the bags and slip them over the clothes hangers.

Regarding supplies you purchase for customers, I suggest including a markup in the prices you charge customers. If you purchase zippers in bulk, for instance, and use one from your stock for a client's order, you should charge the customer for the zipper plus a set charge, perhaps 30 percent of the cost of the zipper. If you pass on the exact cost to the client, you will not be reimbursed for the additional costs of processing mail orders or driving to the store. Additionally, the markup will protect any discounts you might get from suppliers.

# Recordkeeping and taxes

Every business has to keep records for a variety of reasons. In the United States, it's necessary to keep records of all transactions for at least seven years (some accountants recommend keeping them longer). It's important to record the right data, though, or those records won't mean anything.

Because you will need to report all income to the government and pay taxes on any income over expenses, bookkeeping is the most important type of recordkeeping. Be sure to account for everything—every dime that comes in and every dime that goes out. Anytime you buy anything for the business, get a receipt. Sort the receipts per the categories specified on your tax forms. At the end of each day, add up each category of receipts and enter the totals in a notebook. At the end of each month, total each category of expense, and at the end of the year, there will be no more than twelve figures to add in each category. It's that simple.

In order to keep your business and personal expenses and income separate, a business checking account is a necessity. Several years ago my husband and I were audited in a routine periodic audit for sole proprietors. Since I handle all the bookkeeping for both our businesses, I asked the auditor more questions than she asked me! She told me that, for each bank account, the Internal Revenue Service (IRS) determines the total of deposits less withdrawals and then compares that figure to the net income reported on Schedule C. In this way the IRS can see if self-employed taxpayers are fudging their incomes. The auditor advised keeping all business and personal accounting strictly separate, in order to make it easier to keep track of it, and in order to avoid problems with the IRS. In addition, a separate account makes it easier to evaluate the business. If you ever need to arrange for a loan, the business's account activity provides important data for the financial institution that's considering your loan request.

Every check should be deposited. Record what each deposit is for so you will have the same kind of record of income that you have for expenses. This will make it easy to complete your tax return. A self-inking rubber stamp with all your account information will simplify check depositing.

In addition to keeping a separate checking account, have one credit card account that is used for nothing but business purchases. This makes it easier to pay the balance; write one check from your business account each month. It also makes it much easier to see where your money is going; if all the charges are mixed in with clothing and entertainment purchases, it's difficult to separate them. Overly high operating costs are easier to ignore when they're hiding among other expenditures.

# Typical expenses in a one-person or partnership sewing business

- Rent or mortgage (or the proportion of your home rent or mortgage your space represents )
- Telephone
- Utilities
- Office supplies (stationery, software, pens, etc.)
- Sewing supplies (zippers, threads, interfacings, etc.)
- Postage
- Advertising and other marketing costs
- Fees and licenses (checking account fees, professional dues, etc.)
- Taxes, including quarterly estimated income taxes
- Interest on loans
- Depreciation on equipment and furniture used in the business
- Cost of goods (fabric and other raw materials used in your products)
- Mileage
- Insurance

Don't forget mileage costs when you're keeping business records. This is a hidden cost, but it can certainly add up in a hurry. Currently, the IRS allows you to deduct $ .30 per mile—it takes a very short trip to create a $1.00 deduction. In general, you are allowed to deduct mileage for any trip from your home or business to run business-related errands, such as to go to a client's home or to make trips to the fabric store. Even a short trip to the post office or copy store can be business related. Keep good records, and ask your accountant which kinds of trips apply to your particular business.

Depreciation is another hidden cost, and an often forgotten tax deduction. Everything has a useful life, including sewing machines and other equipment: telephones, computers and even software programs. Depreciating this property helps you to spread the cost of these items over a period of time, usually three to five years. The IRS has a list of various depreciation schedules for different kinds of property. What about machines and other equipment you already own? Ask your accountant whether a depreciation deduction is appropriate for you, and if she will prepare a depreciation schedule for you to follow in preparing your tax returns. Your accountant can also advise you whether it is more advantageous to take the entire cost of new equipment in the current tax year, in a special deduction called Section 179.

# Getting advice

Be aware that some businesses take longer than others to show a profit. It may take two to five years before you can get by with no other income. Be prepared for this; many people get discouraged and give up after just a few months. However, planning well and zeroing in on a specialty right away have a positive impact on profitability. Do your market research, seek advice from financial experts and be careful with your spending until you begin to see profit coming your way. Keeping careful records will help you identify ways to improve the bottom line more quickly. If you wait until tax time to analyze the business's progress, it could be too late; your business may already be beyond resuscitation.

Ask other businesspeople who their accountants are, and choose someone from these recommendations. Call the accountant to schedule an "interview" to see if you and she would work well together. (Most accountants do not charge for this time.) Feeling comfortable with the accountant is important; you will share your most personal financial information with her. Ask if the accountant has audit experience; home businesses do get audited, and accountants can accompany their clients to the IRS audit.

Until your business begins to take hold, an initial meeting should be all that's necessary *if* you have your accounting system set up properly. A one-hour session with an accountant at the start-up of your business could be one of your best investments. Inquire about fees, and make an appointment for an hour, with the agreement that the accountant will help you set up your recordkeeping systems.

Make a list of questions for the accountant, and prepare as much information as possible ahead of time. This will help contain costs, and you can spend the time listening to her answers and making notes. Ask for tips on the best methods for keeping your books and what expenses should be tracked. Remember to ask about mileage; this often-overlooked expense is somewhat tricky to calculate.

If you have any misgivings about any aspect of local and state sales or income taxes, this is a good time to seek clarification. Some accountants will even make up a tax payment calendar that indicates when certain types of taxes are due. In some parts of the country, dressmaking and other services are taxable; other places have no such sales tax. Here in Cincinnati, in addition to the quarterly estimated federal income taxes, I also must pay sales taxes at least twice yearly, and once a year personal property tax is due on any business property or inventory. If you hire employees, it adds a whole new set of tax payment requirements.

If your business will carry inventory, inquire about necessary record-keeping and taxes. Inventory has to be counted every year at a certain time, and separate records need to be kept for reporting how much is left at the end of the tax year. Find out how that applies to your business and if inventory is taxed separately in your state.

Be sure to file a federal tax return even if you didn't have income. If you have other income, your business losses can offset your tax obligation and save money for you. Usually filing Schedule C is sufficient, unless you have chosen to incorporate your business (see "Should you incorporate?"). In addition, some businesses qualify for a home office deduction, which may reduce your tax obligation further whether you have additional income or not. Ask your accountant how this should be handled in your case. Be prepared to give her an overall measurement of your home and the square footage of your work space. These figures are necessary in order to figure the amount of deduction.

# Should you incorporate?

Unless your business employs several to many people or manufactures products that may carry a liability, incorporation is often an unnecessary expense. There are filing fees for incorporation plus separate annual taxes. Sole proprietors have none of these expenses. During your meeting with the accountant, check to see what the best business format is for you and for your specialty.

# Insurance

Whether your business is in your home or in a shop, it is always important to protect yourself and your business assets with insurance.

There should be three concerns uppermost in your mind, no matter where your business is located:

- The possible economic loss of property, both yours and your customers'
- Liability, in case someone is hurt on the premises or off
- Ensuring you have enough money to continue in business should you ever have a disaster

Note: Be sure to talk to your agent about what you read here, as laws vary widely between states and provisions vary between companies.

Your first priority is to make sure you *have* coverage for your business. Unless your home business is minimal, a rider on your homeowner's policy is not going to be enough. You need to contact your agent and tell him, honestly, what kind of equipment you have and what quantity of customers' goods are on the premises at any one time.

Why do you need to cover your property? Suppose your home or business were in a fire and you needed to buy all new equipment to get back on your feet. Total how much it would cost to rebuild the business. You might be surprised to find how it adds up. Insurance is meant to put you back in the same position you were in before the claim. An insurance policy that reflects the amount of money you have invested in your business will help you get back to work quicker. If you need to economize, a higher deductible is better than less coverage.

Most companies have a special class of insurance policy called a Business Owner's Policy (BOP), which is designed especially for small companies. These policies are packaged with all kinds of goodies that used to cost a lot extra as add-ons, and they are quite reasonably priced.

One of the special coverages added to the BOP is Customer's Goods, sometimes known as Care, Custody and Control. If a fire or a tornado or another covered event destroys your customer's fabric that's waiting to be made up or her finished goods, this rider would cover their replacement. Consider how useful this would be if you have several thousand dollars' worth of commercial drapery fabric in your workroom or a valuable bridal gown awaiting alterations.

Make sure you get the maximum after a loss, too. Keep good records—photos and receipts—of what you have and *keep them off premises*. It won't do you any good to have meticulous records if they burn up with your business.

# Liability

When you think of the term "liability," sometimes accounting comes to mind, but in this case I'm talking about being liable for an accidental occurrence. Consider the consequences if you were measuring windows or teaching in someone's home and accidentally injured the customer or her child. People sue for that sort of thing. Liability insurance would provide an award to the injured party and other benefits as well.

First, in the case of an accident, you should immediately call the agent and report the incident. The insurance company often offers the injured party an immediate cash payment for any first aid expenses incurred. This does two things: It makes the person who was hurt aware that you care about what happened, and it often defuses any potential difficulty later. Many times, this payment keeps people from suing. Of course, if it does come to a lawsuit, the insurance company will pay the judgment award, up to the limits of the policy. Make sure these limits at least cover your assets, that is, your personal net worth. (To figure this, total all your assets, including the value of your business and business property, then deduct everything you owe.)

Don't worry about losing your insurance as a result of filing such a claim. Accidents do happen, and that's why you buy insurance. Unless you file claims often, a reputable insurance company doesn't cancel for using your policy.

Also included in Business Liability is damage to a customer's property while you're on her premises. For instance, suppose you lose your balance and fall off a ladder while measuring a window. The broken window would be covered under your business policy. (Your injuries would be covered under your health insurance or Worker's Compensation. Check with your insurance agent for how this should be handled, as every state is different.)

If you have employees who sometimes run errands for you, you should specify that they be covered under a liability known as Owned and Non-Owned Autos. This provides protection for you if they have accidents on your time. Be aware, this does *not* take the place of auto insurance.

Another benefit of liability insurance includes the payment of legal expenses should you be sued. As you know, this can be incredibly costly.

Another reason to carry a good insurance policy is to be sure you can get back into business after a serious loss. To insure this, most BOPs cover what is known as Business Income. This provides for a payment by the insurance company of any amounts you would have netted over the period of time your business is unable to operate. (However, you need to supply records of that projected income to the insurance adjuster—another reason to keep records off premises.) Another coverage is Extra Expense, which helps you with other costs of getting back into business, for example, rental of a temporary location.

Other coverages typically included in business policies (but not all, ask your agent if you need one of these):

- Fire Legal Liability: This is important if you rent your space and you cause a fire. Some leases require proof of such coverage.
- Money and Securities, and Employee Dishonesty: These cover you in the event of a robbery or if an employee walks off with your money.
- Accounts Receivable and Valuable Papers: These two riders are very important. They provide coverage to not only pay you what moneys you would have been paid before the loss, but also to recover and restore the records.
- Outdoor Signs: Some of them cost a lot to replace.
- Liquor Legal Liability: If you have a Christmas party or other kind of reception and serve wine, you might need this rider. It covers you in the event one of your guests later has an accident because of partaking of your refreshments.

There are many other policy provisions, but they may or may not be included in your company's policy, as each company differs widely. Also, some states file different versions of Business Owner's Policies than that described here.

## Finding an insurance agent

Be aware that the same agent who handles your home insurance may not know how to cover your business needs, especially if that agent works for a company that traditionally covers mostly family insurance. Ask if there is someone at the agency who specializes in commercial lines. If not, call around to other agencies, either from the yellow pages or from friends' recommendations.

There are two kinds of insurance agencies: the independent agency, where they carry at least two and usually more insurance companies; and the captive agency, who writes insurance exclusively for one company. An example of a captive company is State Farm, whose agents are only allowed to sell that company's products. Usually, captive companies specialize in insurance for families, but not always.

My recommendation is to request a bid from several agents, including one with a captive company if you already have a relationship with it. The benefit of dealing with an independent agent is that he can more easily find a competitive bid for you, depending on the companies he does business with. Also, in case your policy is canceled for some reason, the independent agent has somewhere else to go with your business.

Tell all the agents the same information about your business and the coverage you seek, and ask them to give you two bids: one with exactly what you asked for, the other with their recommendations. This gives you an opportunity to compare apples to apples and allows you to see which agent is willing to listen to you. This is *very* important. Having the right kind of coverage is crucial when you have a loss. In nine years of selling insurance, I saw many policies that had gaps in coverage because the agent hadn't taken the time to get to know the business.

# Copyrights

If you aspire to creating new and different products to sell, be sure these products, whatever they are, are your own creations entirely and do not violate any kind of copyright of another's idea.

This is an extremely volatile area in sewing, in particular because several nationally known companies have begun to vigorously defend their own copyrighted materials. Some companies employ violation spotters, who actually attend craft fairs to find any unauthorized use of their copyrighted images and names. Disney, in particular, has been known to prosecute, which results in hefty fines, seizure of merchandise and lawsuits. Be especially careful of using likenesses of Mickey Mouse, Winnie the Pooh or any other licensed characters. Even the use of fabric bearing these characters is banned, and such a statement is often printed right on the material.

Ideas cannot by copyrighted, but the execution of those ideas falls under copyright law. Just because you change the color of an original quilt

# Dee McCarthy

Dee McCarthy Designs
Park City, Utah

Dee McCarthy's career began before she was even out of elementary school, when a friend of her mother offered her $100 to make a bridal gown for a Madame Alexander doll. That was a lot of money in the early 1960s. Dee continued to sew for others throughout high school and college, earning spending money by hemming garments for other girls in her dorm. "I charged more for rush jobs, even then," Dee says. She graduated from the University of Delaware with a double major in art and art history, then she went into the tour and meeting planning business, although she continued to sew for customers part-time.

After several years, Dee realized the tour business wasn't her calling. She decided to go back to school for a degree in design, and her research brought a shocking revelation: "Schools that teach design don't teach you how to sew. There were thirty students in my class at Harper College [Paletine, Illinois]. Out of this class, only the five of us over age thirty knew how to sew. Not many instructors knew how, either, and I ended up helping to teach the tailoring class."

Dee feels the greatest gift design school gave her was a freedom of design. She says, "I grew up in a conservative area, and these classes helped free my creativity and liberate my design ideas. I still have those designs; it's hysterical to see how the design process opened up. It was fun to see you could take a really good piece of fabric and you could put a little bit of design element to it."

Moving to the resort town of Park City, Utah, has freed Dee further; her clients' larger discretionary incomes free her to be creative in design and allow her to take on different kinds of projects. There are finally people willing to pay what she feels her experience and talent are worth, and now she can afford to do some pro bono, or charity, work. For example, a local public radio station has two fund-raisers a year, and Dee donates a custom ski suit for each event. This has had a side benefit of making her work known to the locals and has given her custom skiwear business a good start.

From the skiwear came other custom work. As Dee is an avid horsewoman, she soon became involved making saddle covers for endurance riders. Then she made leg wraps for Ride & Tie events. This relay team involves three members: two runner/riders and a horse. ("The United States always wins this event in the Olympics," says Dee.) Because the leg wraps, which protect a runner's legs while he is on the horse, have to be removed quickly, Dee designed a special kind of wrap that attached to the saddle. In addition to eliminating the need for the rider to carry the wrap while running, it also made using the wrap more efficient.

"I don't get frustrated by difficult jobs because I often learn in the process; it provides a cheap education," Dee remarks. One alterations job for a wealthy client didn't bring much in the way of hourly income, but it was a distinct learning experience. This couture jacket needed extensive alterations, requiring Dee to unpick quite a bit of the construction. "It was like peeling the petals of a flower," she says. "I learned so much from the handwork in this garment. It was a great learning experience, though it took me twelve times as long as I thought it would. However, because of the job I did with it, this client trusts me with most of her other alterations. For some reason, custom work seems to bring alterations work, rather than the reverse."

Custom work is Dee's first love. This type of clientele uses her service frequently, and they can pay the price for the work. But Dee says there are clients for everyone: "There's a market for $300 bridal gowns, $3,000 bridal gowns and even $30,000 bridal gowns."

Dee also makes custom Polarfleece sportswear, a popular line in her ski resort community. A couple of times a year Dee hosts a home party where she shows her latest styles to interested parties. "My customers enjoy coming to my home, having a glass of wine and some good conversation, and choosing from my line. The benefit to them is they get the colors and styles they want, and the clothes fit them. From my viewpoint, the stretch tights take little time to make, and I do very well with this aspect of my business."

"If you don't learn from it, and you don't enjoy it, you should be doing something else," she says. "I feel very fortunate that I have this business I find so fulfilling, and from which I make a very nice income."

---

pattern, for instance, doesn't mean you haven't violated the law.

In addition, fair use of patterns of others dictates that they are not used to manufacture products to sell as your own creations. The "Big Four" pattern companies, Butterick, Vogue, Simplicity and McCall's, expressly prohibit such use of their patterns.

Commercial pattern companies do, however, allow the use of their patterns in making garments and other sewn articles for customers. Essentially, their policy is this: For each item you make, you should buy one pattern. If you make three dresses from the same pattern for one individual, that's fine, but if you are making the same dress for three different people, you should purchase (or the client should provide) a pattern for each person.

Use of commercial patterns in manufacturing is not only illegal in most cases but also inefficient; cutting apart and using tissue patterns for wholesale manufacturing would be a terrible waste of time. In the industry, oak tag patterns are generally used. If paper is used at all, they are computer-generated patterns printed on the paper in a layout that allows for as little fabric waste as possible. (See the appendix for information on pattern-making software.)

Especially for those who want to manufacture many of something, whether it is a craft, a toy or a garment, the design should be original to you, or you should pay someone to create an original design for that specific item. Many smaller design companies are happy to give you permission to use their patterns, or they will create patterns to your specifications. Some designers ask for a small fee, and others ask simply that you request permission; each has a different policy. This includes designs in magazines; always write or call the publication to get in touch with the designer.

It is a courtesy to ask first; these designers make their living from their designs. Using their patterns for your own gain reduces their ability to profit from their own designs, so be prepared to pay for that right. And never, under any circumstances, copy another's pattern for sale. One woman who did so was levied a fine of $60,000 for attempting to sell six patterns she had copied. A federal marshal who was at the craft show just to watch for this kind of violation caught her in the act of selling them. It just isn't worth this kind of monetary risk. Create your own designs, or find something else to do.

So what do you do if the pattern is from an old book or magazine? If you wish to use such a pattern, at least make an attempt to contact the designer; often the publisher will know how to reach that person. Copyrights belong to the author for many years after her death. In the case of a book that was published in the early 1950s by someone who was thirty-five years old, for example, this copyright would still be in effect long past the millenium. Don't assume that an old book is safe to copy from, except for personal, noncommercial use. "Commercial," in this case, means that you profit by it somehow. These restrictions would also apply to any original patterns you create for sale and protect you from others profiting from your original ideas. Same goes for class handouts; don't copy anyone else's materials without permission, and even then mark the handout clearly to show where the information came from.

Copyright is a tricky part of the law, and this section of the book is not meant to take the place of good legal advice. Please consult an intellectual property rights attorney or the copyright section of the federal statutes at any larger library for more information.

CHAPTER 5

# Basics of Buying and Selling

Anytime you deal with the public you're in a sales situation. Luckily, most sewing professionals don't have many of the problems normally associated with sales. There are few situations where a hard sell is necessary, nor would such a tactic succeed. In general, sewing services are a rare commodity, and the more typical situation is that you have to turn down business than the other way around.

# Overcoming objections

However, there are several basic sales ideas you should know in order to succeed in a sewing business. One is the idea of overcoming objections. As I travel around the country speaking to sewing pros, the questions I get the most begin with, "What do I say when my customers tell me . . ." These are a customer's objections to the sale. Sometimes people just want you to overcome their objections, to give them a reason or justification to spend their money. The only way to get past this is to counter each objection with a benefit to the customer.

- "I can get it at Wal-Mart cheaper."
  **Answer:** "Yes, you can, but it won't be custom-made, just for you, with the fabrics and color and quality you prefer. It won't fit nearly as well, and you might see the same garment on everyone else at the dance."
  **Answer:** "If you could find what you want at retail, why are you here?"

- "Your price is too high."
  **Answer:** "Perhaps I can reduce the price by changing the design. I could delete the lining, which would reduce the price to $X, or I could eliminate the ruffles from the skirt hem." (See the sections on pricing for more help.)
  **Answer:** "I offer a customer service. Your garment will fit only *you*, it will be made in the color and fabric of *your* choice and will include the

67

features that *you* choose, rather than what manufacturers choose to sell this season." (Say this very sweetly.)

**Answer:** "My individualized, custom service should cost more than mass-produced garments, which are made in enormous quantity of inferior fabrics, often in overseas factories by underpaid labor and with lower-quality workmanship."

- "I can make it myself for less than that!"

  **Answer:** "Perhaps." (Period. Don't say anything else. Let her get herself out of *this* one!)

Always answer objections with benefits to the customers, but without being argumentative. Sometimes they honestly can't afford your services, and they really have no business asking you to sew for them to begin with. In cases like these, it's best just to allow them to gracefully bow out of the situations. But be kind; you never know when their financial statuses will change, and then they will think of you first as someone they trust to do that type of work for them. Be prepared to admit that not everyone is a customer—not even Wal-Mart sells to every person who walks into the stores.

Once you have chosen your specialty, these sales situations get easier. You know who your customer is, and he knows you have what he wants. All you have to do is to provide it at a price the broadest range of customers will pay and that gives you the most comfortable profit.

If you develop a patter about your product or service, many of the objections your customers might raise can be quashed before they are ever voiced. You can anticipate the objections forming in the customer's mind as you talk about the window treatments you will make for her, for instance. She might be preparing to complain about having to hang them herself, but when you mention during the course of your discussion that *installation is included,* that objection is satisfied ahead of time, and it dissolves, never to become an issue. This idea can be applied to many other products as well. Shortening pants, for example: Your competitor does them by hand; you have a blindstitch machine that *duplicates the more professional, ready-to-wear method.* Or your stuffed bunnies are *made of genuine mohair, and their eyes are created with safety-locked components.*

When the customer has no more objections, stop answering them. You can literally talk yourself out of a sale by talking too much. Silence is golden, and nowhere more so than in a sales situation. Let the customer make the next move, and if that next step is to say, "I'll take it," all the better.

# Closing the sale

Sometimes you can get to the sale quicker by asking, "When would you like this to be completed? My schedule is open for either May 1 or the following week. Which is better for you?" This is called a close, and there are many ways to close a sale. (See the appendix for recommended reading for more information on selling, or go to the business section of any good bookstore or library.)

# Extra income

Add-on services can make a tremendous difference to the bottom line of your business. Michael LaBoeuf, author of *The Perfect Business*, calls such add-ons PIGs, which stands for Passive Income Generators. For example, alterationist Judy Pagenkopf cheerfully accepts leather repairs, which she then hands off to a leather repairperson who picks up and delivers work to her. Judy pays the repair shop and charges the customer the cost of the service plus a surcharge for handling the repair. The customer doesn't know about the surcharge, but since the leather shop is not generally known to the public, it is unlikely he could access that company. It is not labor-intensive for Judy, so she increases her dollar per hour income by offering such a service.

What type of PIG could you offer your customer? Many drapery workrooms also sell hard-to-find hardware. One designer in Ohio rents crinolines to her bridal and formalwear clients. She also has made up several styles of faux fur capelets that fit over voluminous bridal gown sleeves. Because of the uncertainty of the weather in the Midwest at any time of the year, she makes a tidy income renting these capes to barely covered brides. Another bridal designer also sells satin dyeable shoes to her bridal customers, as well as veils, ringbearer pillows and other specialty items. None of these services take much time to manage.

# Pricing your services

The biggest human temptation is to settle for too little.

Thomas Merton, 1917-1968

As in any other kind of business, how you price your sewn products or services can mean the difference between success and failure. If you overcharge, you might have a tough time finding the customers, especially when the business is new. But underpricing is much more serious. *Not charging enough is the worst pricing mistake you can make.* Businesses with no income at all can survive easier than a business with too little income for the work. There will always be someone with a lower price and someone with a higher price. Don't be the one with the lowest price.

- Underpricing forces you to work harder for less. (If your shop is the busiest one in town, your prices are probably too low.)
- Underpricing taxes your resources; you are too busy, and too tired, to find new income streams.
- Too-low prices tell customers you aren't serious about business. When you pay more for something, you think of it as more worthwhile.
- Underpricing makes your competitors angry and can ultimately pull down all prices in town. Every business will suffer, including yours.
- If you charge too little to begin with, it's difficult to raise prices to the proper level.
- Low prices equal low profit, and thus you can't afford to invest in new equipment and more education.
- The *best* mistake a new business can make is *over*charging.

**Rule of thumb:** If at least 30 percent of your customers aren't hemming and hawing about your prices, they are probably too low.

Karen Howland, the author of *Unit Pricing for Dressmaking*, says, "You're giving up your hobby when you sew for others. If someone asked you to give up sewing for good, what would it take?" This logic helped Karen decide to raise her own prices.

# Pricing strategies

Depending on your specialty, you may have several choices of how to price your products or services.

In the case of craft manufacturing, as much depends on the salability of the product as on the cost to produce it. And if you plan to sell your product to retail stores, prices must be low enough to allow the stores to double that price. Before you begin production, find out if you can make the item cheaply enough to do this and still sell that item. If the item is fairly inexpensive to produce, you can use the "eight times" rule of thumb for pricing: Set the price at approximately eight (sometimes ten) times the amount it cost for the raw materials. If the resultant price is too high, rethink the whole idea. Perhaps it just isn't economically feasible to produce. Or perhaps a different production method or fewer features will increase its profitability.

In order to profit from custom sewing, you need to plan ahead. Use the formula given here to determine what hourly rate you need to charge. I recommend trying to make at least $15 per hour to start; $20 is even better. This gives you a fair margin for overhead, labor and profit. Remember that customers value more highly services for which they pay more.

**Pricing formula**

　　_____ Monthly salary

+ _____ phone

+ _____ utilities

+ _____ rent

+ _____ insurance

+ _____ depreciation

+ _____ taxes

+ _____ equipment/maintenance

+ _____ profit

= _____ monthly income

÷ _____ number of hours worked per month

= _____ hourly price

For dressmaking and other custom services, there are several ways to price. In some parts of the country, you may have to compete more strongly than in other places, and one or more of these methods could be used to give you an edge on the competition.

# Price lists

There are several price lists available for purchase, and you can also use the lists used by dry cleaners and alterations departments. However, you should use these as guidelines only. Some price lists have a strong geographical emphasis; the prices reflected may either be way too high or way too low for your own area and situation. Prices from department stores are sometimes very low, reflecting the store's desire to offer a value-added service to their customer.

If you choose to use a price list as your guide, try to determine what hourly wage it represents. Take some time to change the list to allow you to make what you need to make.

## Garment (or "experience") pricing

Many bridesmaids' dresses are priced by the garment, with a set amount for set types of gowns. This is more a reaction to what the market will bear than any other reason. There are, however, some inherent problems in this pricing method:

- It may take you longer to make garments that others are able to crank out more quickly.
- Certain styles may take much longer than others to make.
- Certain fabrics may be more difficult to sew.
- In the case of experience pricing, you might not remember all the details of the garment you sewed before. Also, each garment and situation have a tendency to differ from one another just enough that it's tough to predict how the project will go.

Susan Khalje, a couture bridal designer who lives in Baltimore, Maryland, feels garment pricing works best for her. After twenty years of sewing for others, she is confident she can predict how long each project will take to complete. She also makes the price high enough that she feels comfortable taking the time to add the couture details she and her customers like best. (For more about Susan, see pages 145-147.)

# Pattern piece pricing

In some areas of the country, every seamstress charges the same amount for the same garment; the price is determined by the number of pattern pieces. For each individual piece of cut fabric, there is a charge of $5 to $15 for labor. However, this doesn't take into account the difficulty of the fabric, so a surcharge is added (20 to 30 percent) for working with slippery satins or tricky velvets. If you use this method, remember to charge for all the pattern pieces used in the lining, too.

A drawback to this method is that it doesn't take into account the skill level of the clothier, nor does it allow much flexibility in pricing the garment. And if there are many fittings, that isn't factored in. One way around this is to charge a flat fitting fee, but that isn't necessarily workable either.

# Hourly rates

Although this method is an excellent way to keep your eye on the bottom line, especially if your sewing is speedy and efficient, it also has some potential pitfalls. First of all, many customers are opposed to paying a set hourly rate; sewing isn't always perceived as a valued service, and if your hourly rate is higher than what the customer feels your service is worth, there may be price resistance, no matter what the rate is. Conversely, if your hourly rate is low, the customer may try to take advantage of your low prices. If you choose to use an hourly rate, avoid revealing the figure to your customers.

Other disadvantages to hourly rates:

- If you are especially slow and methodical, your prices could be impractical for nearly all your potential customers.
- It's easy to underestimate the time it will take for a garment. Since the human body is so complex, a first effort at fitting someone may take longer than subsequent projects for them. And customers tend to downplay the complexity of their projects, both to themselves and to their dressmakers—"It's just a simple dress." (It always is!) Don't be swayed by their opinions—remember, you're the professional here.

If you set up an hourly system, have a timer and a logbook nearby to record every minute you spend on each customer's project. (Having these records can make it easier to experience price later projects and to evaluate your rate periodically.) Be sure to include consultation and fitting times in your log, unless you choose to charge separately for these meetings. But do charge something; your time is valuable, and charging for it communicates that fact to the client.

## Combination pricing

This method combines the garment pricing system and add-on pricing for various details. For instance: A typical jacket with a two-button front, lapels and patch pockets would have a base price. If the customer requests linings, vented sleeves, vent back, welt pockets and bound buttonholes, an additional charge would be made for each of these. This works in the opposite way as well. To save the customer on labor, you can show how stripping these details from the garment estimate will lower the price.

## Pricing for beading

When asked to do beading, be very careful about giving a price. Estimate your time only, and aim for somewhere in the range of $20 to $40 per hour. Beading is very hard on the eyes and is a highly skilled activity. Make sure the customer knows this, and don't sell yourself short by giving a low price for this service.

# Alterations

Pricing alterations is somewhat less complex than pricing custom garment sewing. It's also more competitive in some towns. Using an hourly, or unit, cost works best to develop your own price list.

Begin by timing yourself doing some simple alterations. One expert suggests buying secondhand clothing to inspect and take apart. Practice sewing various types of hems, letting side seams in and out, changing the waist size in men's pants and shortening sleeves. These are the most common alterations, along with replacing zippers and shortening bridal gown hems. (See *Time and motion studies*, page 78.)

Occasionally, dry cleaners or department store alterations departments have price lists posted or available. This might be a good place to start investigating how much is charged for various alterations in your community. Sometimes pant hems are considered "loss leaders," that is, a competitive service to advertise to bring in business. Judy Pagenkopf tries to keep the cost for doing pant hems just about the same as her nearest competitor's charge. The rest of her alterations price list doesn't conform so closely to any other, but it doesn't have to.

# Window treatments and home decor

This is another area where hourly charges work well, but you should probably not call them that. A price list that reflects your targeted hourly income for various kinds of services is normally expected, particularly if you work with decorators as a wholesale workroom. Retail customers don't expect price lists as much as designers do. Designers need to know your cost so they can pass on that cost plus a markup, often 30 to 50 percent, to their customers.

If you choose to act as a wholesale workroom, be especially careful not to compete with the designers for the same customers. Nothing will ruin a business relationship faster than undercutting someone else's price for the same business. Decorators will be more willing to send you business if they know they can trust you. This kind of business is actually easier for you; you don't have to do any of the design, and you don't have to work with the customer or do the installations (unless you choose to do it for the decorator, in which case you should be paid an additional amount).

Most draperies are charged by the width, but there are many variables now with the newer treatments. It would be beneficial to you to keep up with the market by subscribing to one of the industry magazines (see the appendix). These magazines sponsor trade shows around the country all year long, with seminars on marketing, pricing and other workroom issues.

# Embroidery

With the availability of newer, less expensive and more compact embroidery machines, entry into this field is easier and more economical than ever. Many businesses struggle with how to charge for this service, however.

# Beth Hodges

Soft Furnishings
Elberton, Georgia

"I have a gift—I can figure out how to do anything I see. If a customer brings me a photograph, I can nearly always determine how it is made and then duplicate it," says Beth Hodges, who from her home in rural Georgia furnishes draperies, window treatments and all manner of fabric decorative items for the home. About half of her business now is selling "hard" treatments: shades, blinds and decorative hardware. Probably half of her soft business comes from outside her own area. Her tiny community boasts a population of 12,000, with the nearest bigger town about forty-five miles away.

"I wasn't afraid to meet my competitors' prices when I was trying to recruit new business. I told potential customers, 'I charge more, but how about if I use your current price list for six months and we re-negotiate then?' They had been dissatisfied with the service they had been getting, and I met their demands more efficiently. After six months, they were willing to meet my price scale (kicking and screaming all the way!)." As Beth points out, "You have to be prepared to eat jobs sometimes to satisfy customers, and be willing to work really hard to keep their business. A happy customer tells three others; an unhappy customer tells twenty!

"If a customer criticizes others' work in front of you, be careful," she warns, "they will also criticize your work. Never say anything bad about a competitor. And don't say anything negative, especially about the cus-

tomer's home." Beth says many people are insecure about their homes, and your comments may make them even more so.

Beth credits her success in sales to three things: making sure her clients are happy with her work, her advertising and her method of selling window treatments. She advertises in the local newspaper, typically with a photograph of some recent work she has done.

When Beth is selling a treatment, she uses a drawing on graph paper, on a ¼- to 5-inch scale. An exact picture of the customer's window is drawn to scale on the paper, along with the window's relationship to both floor and ceiling. Then every treatment is drawn onto onionskin overlay. The overlays are laid over the graph paper so the customer can see exactly how the treatments will look. "This eliminates so many communication errors," says Beth. "The client doesn't envision puddled drapes, when the treatment I'm showing is actually just floor length. There is a computer program that shows treatments, but it uses a stock window; my method shows the window as it is in real life. I make a sale every time."

"Get it in writing," says Beth about work agreements. Her husband is an attorney, and he advised her to use written contracts, even though under Georgia law a cash down payment is as good as a written document. However, this isn't true in every state, and you should check your own local laws. Beth uses a three-part form and gives one part to the customer at the time of the sale.

Two full-time employees help Beth run her business. On the subject of employees, Beth advises hiring someone with no experience, then training them to do things your way. She says, "I'm not a blamer; I take responsibility for anything that goes wrong, both to the customer and to the ladies who work for me. And I tell them every day that they do a good job."

Beth has a rule for her own and her employees' work: If we can see it, the customer can, too. If it's wrong, do it over. And nothing leaves her workroom with raw edges; everything is finished properly. According to Beth, "We want our products to look custom-made; not homemade and not store-bought. I view everything we do as a stepping-stone to something else, so it's important to make a good impression."

---

Many commercial embroiderers charge by the stitch count of the embroidered design. For example, if the design has two thousand stitches, the cost to the customer would be $2.00 to $3.50 per item, depending on pricing in the area. Up to five colors would be included in this price, with higher prices for more colors. Since part of the cost is in the setup of the design, you could pass on a savings to the customer for multiples of the same design, with price breaks at various points.

An embroiderer in Florida uses the following formula in pricing embroidered clothing items: cost + markup + number of stitches = contract price. It's especially important to include markup (30 to 50 percent) in this type of work so the price includes enough profit to cover other expenses. Because commercial embroidery machines are so expensive to buy new ($3,000 to upward of $30,000), the cost of the equipment should be spread out over the price of the goods embroidered.

# Rush jobs

In addition to charges for services rendered, don't forget about *implied* service. If a customer wants a rush job, charge for it. Many shops charge from 30 to 50 percent additional for rush work; at least one shop charges 100 percent. Remember, if you set time aside from your other work, that makes those other customers wait. Decide what constitutes "rush" for your business: Is it anything that must be completed in less than two to four weeks, or are you willing to take rush orders in less time than that?

Other professions charge a premium rate for overtime; this is essentially what your rush customer is asking for. You may have to work unplanned nights or weekends in order to finish all the work you have to do because of this order. Charge for it.

Do not undervalue your service; that is the worst thing you can do.

# Time and motion studies

In the late 1960s, while working my way through college, I happened to be a time study clerk at a large Ohio factory, Mosler Safe Company. The mere fact that this factory had an entire department for efficiency studies says how important it is to know how much time each operation of a job takes. If you choose to do production sewing, time studies will help you determine how to set your prices accurately and fairly.

To make any money at contract sewing, speed is essential. Speed is usually the result of repeating the same function many times. However, there is generally a plateau where increasing speed levels off and performance remains static. When preparing a bid for a contract job, time yourself performing the same operation at least ten times, then take an average of that function. Calculate all the parts of the job, and use that as your time estimate. And be sure to add in the time it takes to time your work; this is an additional cost to you.

This method will work with making any kind of multiples, whether they are garments, pot holders or awnings.

Tip: When making multiples of anything, it's faster and more efficient to complete one step at a time for the full quantity of items than to complete each garment or project one by one. For example: Add all the sleeves to a pile of doll dresses (all the right ones first, then all the left ones) before adding the collars.

## Get real!

Be sure to use a realistic hourly figure. As appalling as it may seem, some people equate their services with hourly wages in the marketplace. This is unrealistic because hourly employees don't have to pay their own taxes from that money, nor do they have to pay any overhead at all. As a self-employed individual, you are obliged to pay all these expenses and more (see chart, chapter five). If you only charge $5 to $10 per hour for sewing, your actual "income" could be a negative figure! Consider how much it costs to get your car fixed or to have a plumber unclog a pipe. Most sewing pros have at least as much education or experience in their field as these professionals, yet they often have a more difficult time charging for what that experience is worth. Based on that comparison, reconsider your pricing structure.

Charge enough that it is profitable for you to continue in business. If you find yourself saying, "But my customers won't pay that much!" you might want to find different customers. What is the sense of being in business to lose money? Sometimes it takes a few years to get to the point of making a profit; that's different. But if you have been self-employed for a while and have lost money from the beginning, go back to chapter one and regroup. Research the situation and figure out why your business isn't profitable. If "no one will pay," perhaps you should change your focus and find the clients who will pay. They do exist; sometimes you have to shift your sights ever so slightly to see them. Just because no one in your town wears custom suits and evening gowns doesn't mean that no one wears Civil War reenactment costumes or church clothing or specialized leather wear.

# Perceived-value pricing

An alterationist in Florida told me that she charged double the dry cleaners' prices for alterations because she was relatively new to the field. She said, "I tell my customers they have to pay me more because it's hard for me and takes me longer." Her clients have the option of not having her do the work, but they ask for her services. She had the guts to ask for it, so she gets that price. There's a lesson here, I think.

Kenneth King, San Francisco "designer to the stars," author and former cohost of PBS-TV's *Sewing Today*, has my all-time favorite pricing method. King says, "I just figure out what it would cost in retail and add a zero to the end!"

If clients consider your work valuable to them in some way, they are

# Paula O'Connell

**Luxurious Alternatives**
**Oakville, Ontario, Canada**

Paula O'Connell is an accountant who got tired of doing the same thing for so long. She was in a position to do what she wanted to do, without the pressure of having to earn a living, and decided she would rather be an artisan than a profiteer. "Although I do make a profit from what I do, I'm not doing it for groceries. My hobby is self-supporting, and I can work with the quality of materials I want to work with. I couldn't justify buying the latest fancy computerized machine for a hobby, but with the business I could," explains Paula.

"I saw Donna Salyers at a conference in Toronto, and I liked the way the faux furs looked so I bought a kit," says Paula, who, along with many people in Ontario, wears furs. She was sick of replacing them when they wore out, and she was amazed at how well the faux fur wore. "No one could believe it wasn't real, and everyone who saw my coats asked me to make coats for them. I decided to make the coats as a business." She notes, "I'm still doing the fur coats, teaching classes, selling yardage and other activities." Paula feels that if she spent the time to actively market the coat business it could support her without any additional income, although she prefers not to do so at the present.

Paula sells a good portion of her merchandise at consumer shows and one-of-a-kind gift shows for retail stores. She has two children at home, and focusing on shows allows her to concentrate on production and sales without spending a lot of time fit-ting and seeing clients. She has a large warehouse attached to her and her husband's retail display business, so this is where she cuts the furs and sews. They can be messy to cut at home.

Another unique service Paula is focusing on now is dressmaking for cross-dressers. She says there is a market in her area, with no one to serve it, and she feels she is especially qualified to do so. Both her pattern-making training and an open mind allow her to be successful in this type of market. She views it as a costume business.

"Some of these guys want to get a little fussier than the basic patterns or styles available in larger sizes," Paula says. "They want really super designed stuff, some of the same styles they see on the runway." She plans to use her costume, bridal and special occasion wear experience to help her with this specialty, as well as her love of beadwork. This idea also dovetails nicely with her preference for working with one-of-a-kind garments.

Paula has chosen to publicize her business by several methods. One is to send press releases to local newspaper editors. She writes the article herself; many times the paper prints what she submits to them, verbatim. There's a lesson here: Be extra careful about what you submit for publication. "You find out who the editor is, and you send it to that person," she says. "Include everything you want in the article, and don't include anything you don't want to see in print. They won't ask you for permission ahead of time, and they will assume you sent it to be included in the article. Be sure you proofread what you send them first!"

Having an accounting background helps Paula charge what she's worth, she feels. "I know what I have to give up to do this kind of work, so I'm not afraid to charge for that. For instance, it's worth it to me to pay someone else to do my housework, because it's a $7 an hour job. I can spend my time sewing and make more than that," she explains. "You have to figure out how much you want to make in a year and how many hours you are willing to work to make that kind of money. It's nice to say you spent last weekend painting the house, but," Paula asks, "what didn't you do to make that same amount of money? Although, it's hard for me to justify just sewing for money; I have to be able to make really special cre-

ations for a lot of money, to satisfy both my needs."

She reminds others that the cost of machines, power, overhead, full-spectrum bulbs and so forth needs to be factored into the cost of doing business. "You need to charge for it, or you're subsidizing the business. It's hard to do," she admits. You have to ask yourself, "Are you a seamstress, a dressmaker or a sewing machine operator? Choose the skill level at which you are, and decide how much you're going to charge based on your self-description." Paula points out what may seem obvious but often isn't practiced: "More skilled work should command higher prices. Those doing custom work should make more than an operator who is given piles of seams to sew, with no real decisions of fit or style to make."

often willing to pay more. Don't be afraid to think of yourself as a professional—and price your work accordingly.

Note: To reduce price resistance, and to remind yourself of why your prices are what they are, make a poster of this saying, and hang it on the wall of your studio:

The bitterness of poor quality remains long after
the sweetness of low price is forgotten.

Anonymous

# Consignment

A good way for a small business to get started is to sell on consignment to small stores, including boutiques. This means that no money is exchanged until after the items are sold. Usually, accounts are settled once a week, but that depends on the store and how its bookkeeping is set up. Some stores prefer to pay about 40 percent of the retail amount to the designer; others pay as much as 60 percent.

While it may not seem fair that you, the designer, get so little, remember that the store owners have enormous expenses to keep the doors open. In exchange, you get the benefit of their advertising, their yellow pages ads and their excellent retail locations—none of which you had to commit to paying for. Not only that, but the store owners take a chance on anything they put in stock; if it doesn't sell, it gets shopworn and it makes the rest of the merchandise look tawdry. Should that happen, be prepared to again do some honest soul-searching about how well your designs will sell.

Consignment selling is a good way to test the market. If you think you have a hot product, making just a few to sell in a well-placed shop makes better sense than just jumping into a full-scale manufacturing venture. One preemie wear manufacturer in Michigan began her business this way. In three years she has expanded to a catalog of goods she now sells nationally.

# Buying supplies

One of the most important aspects of being profitable involves *not* spending money. Every dollar of income you don't spend becomes profit to you. Reducing your everyday expenses makes sense. Pay less for what you buy.

If you're making articles for customers, try to purchase all raw materials for those products at a price lower than retail. If you pay regular retail for these components, the resulting product will have to cost too much. Finding a better price helps lower your cost, and therefore the price of the item. Maintaining wholesale resources will help contain costs and allow you to maintain a competitive edge in price.

However, sometimes you can be too conscientious of the bottom line.

"I had to learn how to spend money before I could learn to charge for my services," says Karen Howland. "Like many of us, I learned to sew to save money. We mistakenly try to apply our own frugality to our customers, who don't always care to be frugal." Often, when Karen told her bridal clients how much yardage to buy for their projects, she noticed they wrote down more than the recommended amount. "For instance, if a blouse took two and a half yards, invariably the customer wrote down 'three yards.' If I told them they needed four and three-eighths yards for a suit, it amazed me to see them write 'five yards.' " Karen says, "This taught me a lesson and helped make my sewing much more efficient, too. I no longer worried about how to squeeze a layout into a small amount of fabric; this saved me a lot of time."

Knowing that her customers valued her service enough to blow a little money on extra fabric helped Karen place more importance on her own services and charge more for them. Be careful not to ascribe your own values to your customers.

## What are resale numbers?

In order to buy goods at wholesale, you first need to purchase a vendor's license (in most areas) and apply for a resale tax number. This allows you to purchase supplies for the business without paying sales tax, as long as the supplies are to be used in a finished product.

How does this work? Say you manufacture tablecloths. When you purchase bolts of fabric, thread and any embellishments to the cloths, as well as packaging materials, you do not pay sales tax on any of these items, which will all eventually be sold to a customer. The customer, the end user, will then pay sales tax. In most cases (not all, check your community's laws for local compliance), sales tax is meant to be paid by the end user. Whoever is selling the goods collects the tax, then remits it to whatever taxing body demands it. For instance, in my own community the State of Ohio requires sewing professionals to collect state sales tax from anyone who contracts for such services. The business owner then must pay that tax to the state periodically.

No one, except some nonprofit agencies such as schools, is exempt from paying sales tax as an end user. This includes you when you purchase equipment; you are still required to pay sales tax on machines and other items used in your business, even if you have a resale number. Because these items are not going to be sold to someone else (unless you have a retail store selling such items or live in a state with no sales tax), you must pay tax on them.

This is perhaps the least understood aspect of resale numbers, and your insistence on not paying sales tax, if it is required, will earmark you as an amateur. Familiarize yourself with this part of doing business before setting out to buy wholesale goods.

If you are required to collect sales tax, be careful to also then remit the amount you collect to the taxing authority. Keeping that money could be an actionable offense. It just isn't worth going to jail or getting a big fine for the small amount of money typically involved. Keep good records in order to stay within the law.

Many taxing agencies send employees to craft shows to see if all vendors are charging tax. They occasionally purchase goods simply to check compliance. Be aware of such a practice, and make sure you have the proper vendor license or other required documentation.

## Sources of wholesale goods

Finding wholesale sources is one of the most difficult tasks for any business, but in the past it was especially tough for sewing workrooms. Nowadays, with access to the Internet and other resource centers, that part of conducting a sewing business is easier than ever (see the appendix for resource information). You can expect to pay from 30 to 50 percent less from a wholesale resource, typically, with the higher discount available to those who buy larger quantities.

## Pitfalls of buying wholesale

Many wholesale sources have minimum purchases—either a minimum number of yards (of one fabric) or a dollar minimum, usually $100 or more. Some resources waive the minimum purchase amount after the initial purchase, but not all. Don't expect to buy a couple of yards of fabric or a mere package or two of certain notions; that isn't wholesale buying, and asking for special terms for such low quantities is insulting to the wholesaler. Many companies make it difficult to buy from them because they have had home sewing enthusiasts or part-time businesses waste their time with unreasonable requests. Be careful to know their guidelines and stay within them.

Because of the minimums, you may be forced to accept goods in a far larger quantity than you expected to buy. In a case like this, it might be better to purchase the fabric at a retail sale price, or better yet, have your customer purchase the goods. (Note: Many workrooms charge extra for using COM, or Customer's Own Material. This is especially important if the customer brings you unsuitable fabric for a project. Customers also might purchase too little fabric, flawed goods, goods printed off-grain or material that is more difficult to sew.)

Another problem with buying fabric wholesale is that you may have to accept whatever the wholesaler has on hand, even if it's much more than you need for the project. Karen Howland cautions, "Make sure you charge your customer the equivalent of the retail price. Very often when you buy wholesale fabric, the wholesaler doesn't have exactly the amount you need and you're obliged to take more. If you need fifteen yards for a wedding gown, the smallest piece they have may be twenty-two yards— and they don't cut fabric in these places—you get what they have. In this case you would be out quite a bit of money if you had charged your customer the same price per yard you are paying."

Not only are you sometimes forced to buy more than you need, but if there is a flaw in the material, it is more difficult to get a refund or a replacement bolt. And if you've already cut into the fabric and then find a flaw, wholesalers won't take it back at all, unlike some retail fabric stores. Karen says this is also a good reason to take the twenty-two yards; from bitter experience, she automatically adds a couple of yards to her estimate to cover such contingencies. Moreover, if you wait to check the goods until you're ready to cut and sew, there may not be time to reorder. Get into the habit of checking materials right away, to forestall such a situation.

Carol Hawkey, owner of a sewing school in Casper, Wyoming, and publisher of Directions Patterns for children, has some advice if you need a large quantity of goods for a one-time project: "Make the best deal you can with your local fabric store. Minimum, they will give you 10 percent off, maybe up to 25 percent, if you pay up front on the order for one or two whole bolts (usually twenty-five yards)." She further adds, "Think of the risk for the fabric store if you order on promise and then change your mind. They would be stuck with a huge quantity of fabric they didn't want." Thus up-front payment gives them some financial security while it gets you a lower price.

"Manufacturers and mills have huge minimums of several thousand yards," Carol says. "The smallest I've found was five hundred yards, rolled on tubes." A better option for many sewing businesses is to order fabric from a distributor—the ones who sell the folded bolts we're used to seeing at fabric stores. Some distributors have minimums as low as $50, and the wholesale price is about 35 to 40 percent less than you would pay at retail. You will have shipping costs to pay if you order fabric this way, but if your order is large enough, the distributor will absorb the shipping cost. In order to do business this way, you must have a business and a resale license.

Carol advises those who plan to continue to use large quantities of fabric or other goods to start with the *Thomas Register* at the local library. Many fabric distributors (and thousands of other resources) are listed in this mighty reference work of U.S. and Canadian resources. The *Thomas Register* can also be accessed through the World Wide Web. Other sites contain additional European resources and some trade organizations (see the appendix). The Web has many other resource centers as well. Search for *sewing* and any other words that describe your needs: *fabric*, *trims*, *beads*, etc.

# Crafts supplies

Because so many people make crafts casually to sell a piece or two at a time, many suppliers are leery of selling "wholesale." In the past, retail stores, embittered by the hard economic blows sustained when retail superstores opened in their competitive range, complained to suppliers who were selling some of the same merchandise to individuals. They felt business was hard enough to come by without the suppliers "stealing" these sales from them. However, the retailers were also reluctant to sell discounted supplies to crafts professionals.

This has changed somewhat in recent years. A new awareness of the problems of all parties has come about, partly as a result of new professional associations. These groups have sponsored seminars to educate their members on how to buy supplies. By opening the lines of communications on all sides, they have also made inroads in opening the eyes of the various retailers and suppliers to the potential sales these professional crafters represent.

## Attitude is everything

When ordering from a company for the first time, a businesslike attitude is a must. Before you call, have your resale license number, reference addresses and phone numbers handy, and know what you want or are willing to accept. (Of course be realistic about your expectations.) A calm, professional demeanor will go a long way toward getting what you want.

If you write to a company, spend a little extra time to make your "company" look like one. Scrawled messages on scratch paper will be ignored, with some justification. A more businesslike approach will open more doors to you.

Also, if you're unsure about how the sales tax situation works, find out what you're required to do before you call or write to a company about buying wholesale. The local taxing authority usually has brochures or other written material about this, or you can call the Small Business Administration for suggestions about where to get information.

# Contracts 101

Why should you have a contract? Well, consider this true story: A work associate of Julie Davis's husband asked Julie to make costumes for a weekend singing group in Illinois. It was a big order—forty-eight dresses—and the singers were providing the fabric, so Julie didn't ask for a deposit. "I always require a deposit when I am covering the materials; this way I'm only out time and labor, not actual funds, if anything goes wrong," says Julie, who lives in central Illinois.

"We had a measuring session," explains Julie. "I made up the dresses with a loose fit, then I pin fit them in a second fitting session. When they came to pick them up, everyone was twirling around in their new dresses when one of the mothers remarked that the style, which had a fitted, shirred bodice and a flowy, circular skirt, made her daughter look fat." Suddenly everyone thought the girls looked fat, and the lovely garments they had just been admiring on themselves no longer looked as lovely to them. On that sour note, Julie let them take their dresses with them, along with an invoice for the work.

"My contact, who worked with my husband, called a few days after that to say they hated the dresses and they weren't going to pay for them.

Later, we saw promotional flyers all over town advertising the group, and they were wearing my dresses!" says Davis.

"I took a flyer with me to a lawyer for advice. He said it would probably cost as much to fight for the money as what they owed me, which was $3,800, because I would have to sue each singer individually. They didn't have any kind of organized business, unfortunately, or I could have just sued the company," says Julie, who decided to drop the idea of trying to prosecute the group members for the money.

"With a project that big, I wasn't able to work on any other items during that time. When they wouldn't pay me, I not only lost the money from this job, but from any other jobs I might have been doing then." Julie laments, "I really needed that money, too, as I counted on my sewing income to augment my husband's teaching income at the time." Julie feels she learned some valuable, if expensive, lessons from this experience: Never take on a job without a signed and dated contract, always get a deposit and never let the work go out of the shop without getting the balance owed you.

## What is a contract?

A contract can take many forms, but basically it is just an agreement that one party will do something for another party, by such a time and for a specified consideration, or fee. Actually, oral agreements are contracts, but they aren't as easily enforceable as written ones. Oral agreements, in the case of a dispute, often hinge on one person's word against another's, and it's difficult to prove who said what.

One good way to create your own contract is to take advantage of the sample contracts (see the appendix), adding or subtracting parts to suit your own business. Then take the result to an attorney for help in tweaking the document to conform to your local laws. Because laws vary widely from state to state and from country to country, no one document can apply to every situation. Consider having more than one contract if your business offers more than one type of sewing service.

## Why should you use contracts?

Having a signed contract for every job is the ideal situation. Not only will this protect you from your customers' whims, but honest businesspeople should consider their customers' protection as well. If there is a dispute, a copy of a signed contract will go a long way toward showing who might be the injured party. It also keeps misunderstandings to a minimum and makes for good customer relations—everyone knows what everyone else is supposed to do.

Spelling out every detail in a contract also allows you to charge additional amounts for add-on work. Often a customer will decide that a further embellishment or more details or additional parts should be added to the job. This is an excellent opportunity to make a change or addendum to the contract, and you should not be shy about telling the customer this. Have the addendum signed so that both of you know without a shadow of a doubt what this extra work will cost and how it will affect the other details previously specified in the contract.

Having everything in writing also helps you plan your workload in advance. Knowing when projects are due simplifies scheduling additional projects, making it easier to know when to turn down work. Home decor projects, bridal gowns and other jobs that are occasion related sometimes seem to come to you in clumps. Knowing that you are already close to overload will allow you to refer business elsewhere or to leave time open for other possibilities, whether work related or for your own social or family calendar.

Using a contract also sets a tone for the relationship you have with your customers. They know from the get-go that this is a business deal and that you are not just a hobbyist. In short, it saves a lot of energy, in communicating both what you expect of the customer and what the customer can expect of you.

## What a contract should include

- Basics: This is a statement that says who will do what, by when and for how much. Fully describe what these contingencies are.
- Specifics: Spell out who will provide the materials; who will preshrink them, if necessary; what is expected at fittings; what payment methods are acceptable.
- Fine print items: Address what happens if the customer changes her mind—or her weight (brides are notorious for changing dress sizes).
- Policy sheet: This includes your "rules."

## Policy sheet

This is an addendum to the contract that further details your expectations of the customer and what he can expect from you. Have the customer initial each section as you review the information together at your initial meeting.

- When the raw materials need to be delivered
- When the first fitting or measuring is scheduled
- What clothing, shoes, undergarments, etc., are to be worn to the fitting
- How checks or charges are handled (including your policy on bounced checks)
- How payments are to be made and when
- Amount of deposit expected for different types of work
- Suggested calling hours, appointment times
- Cancellation policy
- How missed or late appointments are handled

Like the contract, the policy sheet shows the customer you are a serious businessperson. It reduces the possibility of misunderstandings. However, should any arise, having the customer's initials on the policy sheet should help smooth over any problems. (See a policy sheet example on page 150.)

# Show me the money!

## Consultation fees

Many dressmakers and tailors charge consultation fees for initial meetings with new clients. This fee is later applied to the cost of any work performed for that customer. This practice helps you to establish from the beginning that your time is worth money, and the customer is less likely to waste valuable minutes for you. If you're like Kim Lawrence, who likes to chat with her drapery customers, it will also keep you from wasting your own time!

# Joyce Murphy

JSM Tailors
Bainbridge Island, Washington

Joyce Murphy

For nearly twenty years, Joyce Murphy has been tailoring designs and altering tailored apparel. After creating career wear from her home for four years, Joyce moved to her current shop in 1985. She sold made-to-measure suits for eight years and employed an in-house wardrobe consultant. "I kept looking for ways to provide career wear for women and had hoped to work into the custom area," she explains, "but I don't like not being paid for the time to shop for fabrics, and now I've stopped making custom, as well as the made-to-measure. The business wasn't growing on its own because of the dress-down trend of the nineties. I would have had to beat the bushes for business, and it wasn't something I wanted to do."

Now Joyce focuses on alterations and tailoring. She has spent a lot of time revising her price list and making it work best for her business. She does show this to her customers if they want to see it. It gives her a backup, and since the list looks quite official, it offers credibility to her pricing structure. Prices reflect the different methods required, especially the variances between men's and women's alterations techniques.

"At Seattle Central Community College, I took classes for my apparel design degree from a tailor." Joyce says, "I use that course more than anything else I took; it was extremely beneficial." There are standard ways of altering certain types of garments in menswear, and Joyce says many people aren't aware of them. "I think there's a real need for this level of understanding tailoring." She notes, alterations done in this manner turn out better, and use simpler, more cost efficient methods. But most dressmakers who have a home sewing background aren't aware of these techniques. Joyce feels that the ability to do alterations helps anyone doing custom work to fit better. The difference between the professional and the amateur is that the professional follows through on the garment, taking the extra time to make it fit properly.

Owning a storefront allows Joyce to lend a helping hand to the other sewing pros in her small island community in Puget Sound. Joyce hires others from the area to work in her shop and showcases local talent in her shop's window. "I feel the impor-

tance of providing serious part-time work for talented employees," she says. "Not everyone wants the responsibility or time commitment of owning a shop. In a time of corporate downsizing, one of my goals is to 'upsize' sewing businesses." As part of JSM Tailors, these part-time employees are on-site for referrals when customers ask for work that Joyce doesn't do. Paula Shelkin, who works for Joyce three seven-hour days a week, says she gets about 80 percent of her home decor business as referrals through JSM.

Joyce has set up a payment system that allows the employees to share in the income from the pieces they alter. "Every alteration requires both fitting and sewing, so I pay employees 42 percent for the sewing done, 14 percent for the fitting. That adds up to 56 percent, and there's another 5 to 6 percent in payroll taxes, so we're up to about 60 percent." And, she adds, "There's another amount of cost in zippers, thread and other parts and pieces that go out the door with the garment, about 5 percent. This is all added into the cost of goods. So my gross profit margin is about 35 percent," which is what she aims for. Joyce also points out, "With increased volume, I pay slightly more, because the basic costs don't go up. I pay a quarterly bonus based on the percentage of sewing work done by each person."

Joyce enlists the help of her employees to make her business profitable, in a system sometimes known as MBO—Management by Objectives. She also runs her business in an open book accounting method; the employees all know how the company is doing every month, and everyone strives to help maintain a healthy profit picture for the business. Joyce pays herself an administrative wage to make up for the training she gives the employees and the bookwork she must do to keep the business running.

Joyce does get help doing the payroll forms, but other than that she does everything herself in a Lotus 1-2-3 spreadsheet and pays bills with Intuit QuickBooks. She says, "I do a profit and loss statement with the help of these programs so I know how my business is doing. You have to under-

stand the bookkeeping part, otherwise how can you track your progress?"

Joyce adds, "Specializing in one or two things makes it much easier because then each business has its own slot for expenses, etc. From a bookkeeping standpoint, it's much easier to run a singularly focused business. You understand what you're doing, and can make it better." The same applies to your specific jobs. She explains, "If I'm hemming jackets and I get them five days a week, I'm going to get faster at it. If I see one a month, it isn't quite the same. We do want to see variety, though, to keep our interest."

## Deposits

When you take on a job, it is wise to get a deposit before starting the work. Kateri Ellison, like many dressmakers, never begins new work without a 30 percent deposit. In some specialties it may be necessary to charge 50 percent to start a new job, especially if the work requires special equipment. Rule of thumb: Specify in the contract how and by whom the upfront expenses will be covered, especially fabric costs to you. All deposit provisions should be negotiated and spelled out in the contract.

## Final payment methods

Never release work without a final payment; as Julie Davis's contract story so painfully illustrates, you may never be paid for the job. Sometimes buyer's remorse sets in and your customer is reluctant to pay for what may have been an impulse purchase he couldn't afford. Special-occasion garments are notoriously subject to nonpayment, especially after the big event is over. Or a spouse finds out how much something cost and forbids payment. This is a touchy situation; you deserve to be paid for your work, and you have no control over the client's marital or domestic situation. In cases like this, contracts are your only way of proving you are owed the money.

Many brides are so preoccupied with the flurry of getting ready to be married that they forget they have closed their checking accounts. It is unwise to take a check from a bride the day before her wedding!

If you never release work without payment and always require a deposit up front, you will only lose the profit part of the payment. This isn't an optimal situation but is better than not being paid at all.

### Final payment options

- Payment by check one week before release of work (or however long it takes checks to clear with your bank)
- Money order or cash, then release
- Check payment, then release
- Credit card payment, then release

In the case of a bounced check, you should definitely pass on the fee to the customer. Your bank charges you for this, and you shouldn't have to absorb that cost just because the client is a lousy money manager. Find out what the fee is, and post a sign that says "Returned check fee: $XX." (Many banks now charge as much as $40 per check.) Add this same wording to your contract, in the fine print area.

# Credit cards

In the case of a large installation for window treatments, it may be necessary to ask for final payment at installation. In this industry and for other specialties with large financial outlay by the client, access to merchant credit card services is beneficial. Check with your bank to see if such a service is available to your business.

Most banks require a business to show them some sort of track record indicating sales strength before they commit to issuing a credit card service. Be prepared to show financial records of at least one year; some banks require two years' information. To ensure payment of the costs involved, banks require companies with credit card services to set up accounts in those same financial institutions. These may be merely DBA, or Doing Business As, accounts, which are lower-cost checking accounts that normally don't pay any interest on the balance. Because true business checking accounts can be costly, this is an economical option for a small business. The credit card costs are then transferred directly from the account; and the transaction deposits, directly to the account. Because there is no waiting for the deposit to clear, the businessperson has the money in the account within twenty-four hours of when the deposit is made.

## Protect yourself

If you follow all the steps I've described, your chances of success will be greater than if you run your business haphazardly. For businesses that begin slowly, these procedures are sometimes difficult to segue into, but the rewards are great for taking the time to put these precautions into place. There may still be times when you are forced to consider a customer's account a dead loss. In such a case, remember you can take the amount as a business loss deduction. Ask your accountant how this should be handled.

Also, sometimes it just isn't worth fighting for a few dollars. The lesson learned may be worth the money lost, in the long run. As Julie Davis says, "I learned many things from my experience. I look at this as a lesson I couldn't have gotten anywhere else." There are very few classes in sewing business management, and though experience can be a painful teacher, here's an optimistic thought: Experience can also offer a relatively inexpensive education.

# CHAPTER 6

# The Business Plan

Having a plan is always a good idea, whether you're plotting out your future business or just going on a picnic. Consider the consequences of beginning a trip without consulting a map: Who knows where you'd end up? The same is true of a business: Unless you have some idea of your objectives, your energy will be too scattered to accomplish your full potential.

In a start-up business, having a plan can make an enormous difference in how quickly the business fulfills the owner's goals. However, even existing businesses benefit from a business plan. Taking stock is a good thing to do, especially if the business seems to be stagnant, or if profit is low, or if the owner is so busy working she doesn't seem to have any other life. Developing a business plan forces a redirection of energy, one way or the other.

# What is a business plan?

Despite the official-sounding name, a business plan is nothing more than a list of actions. Call it an action plan, if that sounds friendlier. This plan outlines all the steps needed to get a business going and to keep it running smoothly. It spells out the goals of the business owner and affords a "track to run on," or a road map for the business. It helps keep the owner from wasting time and energy doing anything that won't move the business forward.

Your business plan should provide, in whatever form you desire, a list of priorities and plans for your business future.

## Action list

This list details the first things that need to be determined.

## Where will the business be located?

- Are there any local zoning problems? If so, can anything be done to change them?
- What changes to that location need to be made?
- If the business will be in your home, does this mean some remodeling should be done?
- Is the location convenient for customers, if they will come to you?
- If the business will be in a "street" location, is one available? What kind of lease is required, and do you need to hire an attorney or real estate agent to help with this?
- Is any furniture needed to create a comfortable work environment?

## Is your skill level up-to-date?

- If not, what needs to be done to get up to speed? Classes, or an apprenticeship? Where can these be obtained?
- What do you know about the specialty you picked? Will networking with other professionals help?

## What kind of help will you need?

- If your business needs additional employees, are there possible candidates in your community, or will you need to train people?
- Will you need professional help, such as an accountant, lawyer or other specialist? Where can this be obtained?
- Is there an SBA office in town that can provide additional business assistance?

## What kind of licenses or permits are required?

## What state and local ordinances and laws do you need more information about?

- What is the current information about sales taxes, income taxes and any additional requirements, such as labeling laws, in your area?

## What equipment do you need?

- Can it be obtained locally, or do you need to find other sources?

- Can this machinery or equipment be serviced easily, or do you need expert service? Where can this service be found?
- What kind of supplies do you need for this equipment? Where can they be obtained?

**What office supplies do you need?**

- Can these be obtained locally, or is a mail-order source needed?
- How about business cards and stationery? Will a simple design suffice, or would you like to hire someone to design a logo and use more interesting paper supplies? Whom will you hire?
- How will you handle paperwork? Can you get by with boilerplate forms, or will you create them from a computer program? Do you have a computer, and do you know how to use the program?

These are just suggestions to get you started; it's important to carefully evaluate your own needs and adjust your action list accordingly.

# Your business time line

Decide when everything on your list needs to be completed. This doesn't have to be a hard-and-fast date unless you want it to be, but it helps to have some kind of target. If you never make a goal, you won't ever complete all the tasks.

The simple act of committing a date to paper helps to establish it in your mind. It's surprising how powerful this action is. Try it and see how it works for you.

# Business specialty: Who are you?

As discussed in chapter two, having a specialty defines your business. It keeps you from wasting time and energy doing anything that doesn't forward the goals of your specialty.

Also, when you have a specialty it makes it simple to know what to list on a business card. This is helpful when you're getting started; every card and every marketing device will say who and what you are, right from the beginning.

# What's your name?

It's all in a name, and your business name should give a clue as to what your business is about. Even something as simple as "Mary's Tailoring" is sufficient, as long as it tells what you do. A good name defines your business, just as a specialty does, and eliminates time-wasting phone calls.

It amazes me how many different ways there are to cleverly use the word *sew* in a business name. However, there is a limit to possible combinations, and someone else may already be using an idea that comes to you in a dream some night. Most states allow you to register your business name so there won't be more than one business with the same name; some states allow you to use your own name without registering, as in "Karen Maslowski School of Sewing." Contact the local SBA office for information on what the laws require in your area.

# Your target market

If you have chosen a specialty or a couple of areas in which to specialize, it's easy to figure out who your target market is. If you've chosen to make wedding gowns, you already know that parents of young children will be less likely to need your services than will college-age women or younger businesswomen. However, a less likely, but probably beneficial, place to advertise custom bridal work is in a community of older, more settled people: They often have daughters and granddaughters who may need your services. (See chapter nine for more information on advertising and marketing.)

Knowing who your target market is helps to further focus your attention on that group of individuals. Get to know them and their needs, and offer them solutions to those needs.

# How to reach that target market

Once you know who you want to reach, determine where to find them. This is not always easy, and sometimes takes a little detective work on your part. Include in the action plan how you intend to get your message to these potential customers.

# How (and what) to charge

These are two different things—how to charge may actually be more important. Review the pricing methods described in chapter six. Decide which you will use and how much you need to charge to make a profit. Include the whole gamut of pricing situations in your action plan.

# Where to get supplies

What supplies are available wholesale, and which do you need to make arrangements to purchase locally with a discount? Try to have this information written in your business plan.

# Equipment needs

Is your current equipment sufficient for your business, or will you need to expand in the near future? If you need more equipment, where can you get it, how much does it cost and who will service it? Estimate how long it will be before the business can afford to make such a purchase.

# Expansion plans

What will this business look like in six months?

- How do you think you want to do business in the future?
- Do you always want to do the same thing, or would you like your business to evolve somehow?
- What kind of income do you want in six months? Do you hope to break even by then? Write it down; it won't become reality unless you have a plan.

# Future plans

Where do you want to be in one year, five years, ten years? Maybe you would like to be on the beach in Cancun. Who wouldn't! But maybe you'd like to have a staff in a few years so you can still have the business *and* take a vacation periodically. Would you hope to have a specific annual income at a certain future date? This is the time to plan for it and write it down.

Do you have a finite plan, to accommodate a particular life goal? Perhaps you only want your business to continue until a certain date or event.

- The kids are in school or in college or still at home.
- Your spouse retires.
- You get divorced or married.
- Your house is paid off.
- You win the lottery!
- You _____ (fill in the blank).

## Plan for personal and business growth

This is very important: Be sure to include plans for your own development. Whether you want to take classes to improve your skills or join support groups, be sure to accommodate these interests. And don't forget to make time for social activities. Remember, all work and no play made Jill a very dull girl.

That's it, that's all there is to a business plan. Just because it's on paper doesn't mean it's set in stone, however. You can always change your mind—it's *your* business! But for now, this is your plan. Review it periodically, as your goals and business needs change.

# Catherine Bennett

Carina
Kirkland, Washington

Catherine Bennett

In late 1992, after a sixteen-year career in interior design, Catherine Bennett initiated her custom design line, Carina, in her home in Kirkland, Washington. Her plan was to provide the type of clothing she herself had trouble finding: well-fitting, smart, career wear of natural fibers, coordinated in groupings of pants, skirts, jackets and blouses. Bennett had a lifelong interest in sewing for herself, and she had taken classes in fashion design in the late 1980s, including some patternmaking courses. She thought she could make this type of clothing for fellow professionals and they would fit everybody.

Word-of-mouth referrals from her colleagues from interior design brought in the first trickle of clientele. Then her first big break came in February 1993, when a feature article about her new business was published in the "Scene" section of *The Seattle Times*. Customers from these two kinds of referrals made up her core clientele. "The news articles were most successful as far as marketing—this is the kind of advertising you can't buy," Catherine says. "Fashion shows weren't as good for me; the ones I did were too expensive to put on, with space rental, guest speakers, refreshments, invitations, programs and the expense of creating two dozen garments. Some shows ended up netting nothing at all." Another good way to bring in business was sending brochures out to names from a mailing list she purchased. This list included women in the vicinity who made under $100,000 a year. At $1 a brochure, plus mailing costs and the expense of the list, this was less expensive than other types of advertising, although still pricey.

As to the division of labor, Catherine created the designs, then hired a patternmaker to correct the fit, fine-tune the patterns, then grade for different sizes, usually from size 2 to size 12. Catherine also did some of the patternmaking, sewed, supervised, cleaned, serviced machines, did the marketing and made the sales. In addition, she also purchased fabric for the line each season. There were usually three to four other employees who assisted with production and other tasks. Catherine's husband, Dan, did the paperwork for the business, including payroll. "I paid my employees quite well,

and they were all excellent. If I had it to do over again, though, I wouldn't have employees," she now says. "It was expensive, and I had to constantly work to keep them busy. It was insane."

In fact, Catherine admits she made many mistakes, and she hopes her story helps others who want to produce clothing. Although she had been self-employed previously, she realizes now that she didn't have the right kind of business experience to make the business successful, and it has taken her several years to learn hard lessons about developing a line vs. making custom clothing. "I thought it would be easier than it is. You don't need formal education, but you do need to know more than I did," says Catherine. "Our customers, like everyone, had lots of fitting problems, and each garment had to have a custom pattern. Contrary to what I originally thought," she recalls, "every fabrication required a new pattern, because different fabrics had to be fit differently. It took about eight to ten hours to develop a pattern, then make a muslin and then do the fitting. It was hard to get enough for a custom garment to cover those costs." Although Catherine had a stated pricing policy, it was not adhered to, and she admits, "This was a mistake—it cost me money as well. We couldn't price our line high enough to cover these costs— fitting time and client contact alone took from three to five hours. My jackets were around $500 to $700 apiece, but this wasn't enough for the quality of workmanship, and the time and care spent in making the garments fit." Some customers thought Carina's prices were too high, saying there wasn't a designer label. Catherine says, "It made no difference that my garments were equally well made, one-of-a-kind and custom fitted. Not only that, but they were made in the U.S., by hourly employees." It was difficult for Catherine, an admittedly poor self-promoter, to overcome customers' objections (see chapter six) and educate them to see the benefit in buying from her, as opposed to buying goods made overseas with exploited labor.

Other mistakes Catherine feels she made: purchasing too much fabric (she still had $15,000 of fabric in inventory at the beginning of 1997); hiring a rep who didn't have Catherine's best interests at heart; and having her business in her home. As she points out, "There's no walk-in traffic in a residential area; your customers have to plan to be at the studio. I had no way of getting accidental business."

Catherine offers this advice: "Don't fly blind like I did. Do your homework; talk to other designers and other people who are doing similar things. Make a plan." She also feels there isn't anything wrong with hard work, but you do have to eventually get a reward for it.

# CHAPTER 7

# Financing the Business

Any business needs money to start with, if only to pay for a few supplies. How to find this money depends on how much you need, plus a variety of other factors.

First, determine what your needs are, based on the decisions made while creating a business plan. Then use the following methods to decide how to accumulate the capital to get started.

# Financing a business

There are two ways to finance a business: with your own money or with someone else's money. How much capital is needed and how much is on hand will have as much bearing on this decision as anything else.

## Bootstrapping, or "baby steps" method

A common term in small business circles, "bootstrapping" refers to using whatever resources are on hand to make the business grow, then pouring any profits back into the business. What are the advantages of doing this? First of all, there's no need to go through any formal loan proceedings. If you began the business to add a little extra income to the family, the added burden of debt is generally not desirable. It may also be the only option, if your credit record is less than sterling.

When I started my sewing school in 1987, I used a small nest egg I had accumulated. This allowed me to invest in sewing machines and even to remodel the part of the house where the school was to be. I didn't have to pay anyone back but myself, which I did within a few short months. I used new income to purchase additional supplies and equipment and to beef up the minimal initial advertising my meager budget allowed. This method worked well for me; I didn't want to grow quickly. Too many students at once would have been too overwhelming; this slow beginning gave me a chance to figure out the best way to run the school.

With this method, new equipment and other upgrade decisions are made based on what kind of income the business is getting. The use of existing equipment and supplies pays for new purchases. If business is slow, it may take longer than planned to achieve all of the acquisition goals you have. It may mean your business grows even more slowly, without the added push a yellow pages ad or a faster industrial machine might provide.

Many people in sewing businesses get their start this way, with a minimum outlay of start-up capital. The advantages are many: No loan to pay back; the business can use the machines and other equipment already owned; and there is less pressure to immediately make lots of income. There is a disadvantage, however: If your business idea is so hot that it takes off right away, you could be facing an immediate crisis not being fully operational from the beginning. As you work on your business plan, decide whether or not this is something that will give you trouble.

## Financing, or the "giant leap" method

One of the major causes of business failure is lack of capital, not only for start-up, but for covering day-to-day expenses. When a business is financed from day one, it gets a head start at success. From the first day, the owner has the money to pay for advertising, new and up-to-date equipment and a business phone line.

A danger of financing is that the business may take a long time to succeed, and the intensity of the need to make a loan payment each month may be more pressure than you want to accept. Having the business start out "in the hole" financially sometimes makes a difficult obstacle to overcome.

Also, the learning curve of new equipment and methods may counteract any benefit of starting out so well equipped, unless you can get training first. If after you have worked for awhile you decide you don't like the business, you could be stuck with unneeded equipment plus debt that isn't paying for itself. Think this through carefully before considering financing.

If you decide you need to have more capital than your own reserves can provide, dust off that business plan and head over to your local bank to arrange financing. Be sure this version of your plan is typed and legible. Your banker can tell you whether or not he needs any further information.

One thing he will probably want to know is how much income you project each year for the next five years or so. The bank will also want to know the particulars of your personal finances: how much money you owe for loans; the amounts of mortgage and equity on your home; estimated monthly bills; and any financial assets you own, including life insurance, retirement accounts, investments and personal property.

An alternative to bank financing is that old standby: Mom or Dad. Borrowing from a family member is a time-honored tradition, but tread carefully in this mine-filled territory. Be conscientious: Use a written contract and be ultracareful to make the payments you say you'll make. And be prepared to accept unsolicited advice: It's an unwritten law that anytime you ask parents for money, you automatically invite their interest in your life. If you don't take advantage of them, hopefully, they will return the favor.

# How to decide which method of start-up to use

Questions to ask yourself:

- How much of a risk taker are you?
- How strong is your market?
- How refined are your skills; will there be a period of learning?
- How much stamina do you have, both for the work and for the concept?

## How much of a risk taker are you?

A typical entrepreneur profile seems to indicate a penchant for risk taking, but that's not always the case. Many business owners would prefer to plod along and keep the money they make without taking any kind of scary gambles. Others prefer the thrill of taking an idea, throwing caution to the wind and building it into a fabulous empire. Perhaps you fall somewhere in between these extremes.

My husband, Steve, also has his own business. He's a conservative person, hates to spend large amounts of money and refuses to have any kind of installment debt. It just makes him too uncomfortable to think it might not be paid. I, on the other hand, sometimes like to plunge right in with ideas and tend to look less at the bottom line than at my visions of success. Naturally, our styles clash occasionally. Steve would prefer that I didn't spend so much money up front sometimes, and I have encouraged him to deliberate a little less about major equipment purchases that would pay for themselves in better time efficiency and higher-quality output. And I make sure I have enough cash to purchase any new equipment or service for my business. Talking about this over the years has benefited both of us: We each have a more balanced risk-taking profile as a result of the other's influence.

You have to decide your own level of tolerance of installment debt, which can be critical in any business. Consider other alternatives if it would be too uncomfortable for you to finance your sewing business. Perhaps you could sell an investment or other property, trim certain expenses or scale back your plans somewhat.

## How strong is your market?

Again, if the market is there for your product or service, and if waiting until you have the money saved could cause you to lose a timing advantage, financing would probably be a good idea for your new business.

On the other hand, if you're not sure whether your heirloom christening gowns will be an immediate hit, a slower start is probably a safer business bet.

## How refined are your skills?

If there will be a period of learning, you might want to operate such a business part-time for awhile, until you're more comfortable with the process. The computerized embroidery business is a good example. According to a professional embroiderer, there is a high potential even for experienced machine operators to damage embroidered garments. Learning to use the machines could mean a big difference to the profit picture of a commercial embroiderer. Also, having designs digitized for embroidery can be costly; learning to do this service yourself could also shave costs.

## How much stamina do you have?

What kind of staying power do you have? Can you sustain your interest in this idea long enough to pay off a loan? Will the work entertain and interest you that long? Or will you be bored with it, but stuck with a seemingly endless string of payments?

# Hiring professional help

When you are setting up the books for your business, you can ask your accountant for advice on financing. An accountant can also help you refine your business plan so it conforms to any guidelines your lending institution may prescribe.

## Partnerships

If you decide to start a business with a partner, be sure to consult both an accountant and an attorney. Under no circumstances, even if the other person is your best friend or close relative (perhaps especially in those cases), enter into a partnership without formal partnership documents. Many lawyers go as far as counseling their clients to never enter into a partnership. Some professional advisors suggest incorporating as a way of limiting potential problems, as well as personal liability.

## Liability

Most small sewing or craft businesses work best as sole proprietorships. Unless your product line has a liability exposure or you have several employees, incorporation is probably unnecessary. Examples of products that might require protection from liability suits are baby carriers, some types of toys, protective garments (for firefighters, police officers or auto racers, for example) and parachutes. This is by no means every possible product with exposure to product liability lawsuits. Consider how your product will be used, and make sure your professional advisors, including insurance agents, know of any pitfalls related to your product's use. Be sure to have adequate insurance—and be aware in advance that such high-risk coverage can be costly.

# Kitty Stein

**Workroom Concepts**
**Clearbrook, Virginia**

Kitty Stein

Kitty Stein began her career in a department store that made draperies and slipcovers in its home fashions department. She was there for two years and realized there was no chance of advancement. She was bored sewing only drapes, so Kitty began making window treatments from her home for another designer.

"At the time, 1978, I didn't think of this as a 'business'; I thought it was fun, and I could make some money sewing. The designer taught me quite a bit; she had had a workroom for some time, and already had a price list," says Kitty.

"After about a year or so, she suggested I hire someone else to help out. I put an ad in the paper and hired someone. The day Nancy came to work for me," Kitty says, "it occurred to me that I should check with my attorney to see if my home was zoned for employees. He said it wasn't, so I fired her the same day she started working." After that, Kitty's attorney arranged it so both Kitty and Nancy operated businesses from Kitty's home, and the customers paid them each directly. "Sounds good," says Kitty, "except I wasn't smart enough to make any money from the situation. I was training her, and she was getting the benefit of everything I knew, but I didn't get reimbursed for my part in bringing her work. It didn't dawn on me that I should get a little more for training, and my attorney assumed I knew to do so."

Things changed in 1980 when Nancy and Kitty became partners. "We had industrial sewing machines and a lot of other equipment, all in an 11' × 16' room," recalls Kitty. "We bought all the equipment the salesman told us we needed; he told us we could make all kinds of money because the equipment would increase our production." The salesman was right, but soon the partners worked themselves out of jobs and had to implement marketing strategies and canvass for new customers. This was something they really didn't want to do or know how to do. Retailing to individuals was not their intended focus.

"One of the best things we did was to have a professional brochure made, describing our services; it gave us something to hand to potential clients. We went to the Washington, DC, area and walked into businesses, literally knocking on doors." As Kitty tells it, "I remember walking into a fabric store, hiding behind bolts of fabric and arguing about who *had* to go talk to this person. We didn't know what we were doing; it's hysterical to look back on it now and remember this. We actually walked out of some of them with work, and I have no idea how we did that!"

Business did start to come in regularly, and the two decided to move into a store. "Again, we didn't consult with any of our consultants; we just told them after the fact." Kitty says, "Our accountant about had heart failure. He said we didn't have enough income yet." But the partners thought the price was right and rented a 6,000-square-foot store. Since it was more space than they needed, they set up part of it as retail space and hired decorators. "We had no experience hiring, so we hired everyone who applied," which could have been costly, but, Kitty says, "Fortunately, we were paying them on commission, so we didn't have to pay them unless they sold. However, we didn't know how to sell, so we couldn't teach them how to sell. To actually get Mrs. Jones to sign on the dotted line was harder than just handing over what she came in for."

Nancy handled the retail business, and Kitty managed the wholesale business. Though, according to Kitty, "Neither of us had any business managing. We were sewing at first, and eventually we hired as many as four seamstresses. That was a problem. We both got into the business because we loved to sew, but with all our responsibilities we didn't have time to sew anymore."

By the end of 1990, both of them were weary. "Nancy was tired of the employee problems that had begun to spring up with a couple of our decorators, and I was tired of the whole thing," says Kitty. "We decided to close the business, rather than to sell it. Nancy kept the van, and she has her own installation business now. I kept the equipment, and did work for designers from my home."

At this point, Kitty was hoping to share her business experiences by writing about them. "I spoke to the editor at *Draperies and Window Coverings* magazine, who asked me to send them a proposal. I sent it, along with ideas for about six articles, and they said 'write it.' They haven't told me to stop, so I'm still doing it," she says. "I write about the kind of information I wish I'd had, and I hope it helps others from making the kinds of mistakes we made." Kitty also presents seminars for the magazine and consults with people setting up window treatment businesses. She developed a packet of forms for photocopying for drapery workrooms. These forms can help workrooms with ordering, measuring, pricing and many other day-to-day operations. Kitty also writes a regular column for *SewWHAT?*, a newsletter for drapery workrooms, and she is a regular contributor to DraperyPros, an e-mail list with a weekly

online chat (see the appendix for more information).

Kitty's advice to those interested in succeeding in a sewing business: "Research what you want to do. Be prepared, businesswise, for the roadblocks, because they're going to be there." She emphasizes, "Educate yourself, so you're prepared for it. If you have employees, you especially need more information. And when you learn something, be willing to share with others. It will make the road easier for someone else, and will make us all more successful." You need to realize you're in a business, and that you are selling something. Kitty knows now that you can't expect to learn everything at once; the education process is ongoing.

Kitty feels the most important step toward success is to plan ahead. "Make time to plan; know where you want to go. Don't just let your business take you wherever." She says, "If you don't know where you want to go, you won't know what kind of education you need to get there." Kitty says she made goals for each upcoming year, then didn't think about them again until the following year. "I did part of it, but didn't take it far enough. You need to lay out all the steps it will take to get to your goal. If you don't get focused, you don't get real good at one thing, or a couple of things. And you won't get the reputation you need to further your business."

# CHAPTER 8

# Advertising and Marketing

"There's a difference between *work* and *business*," says Karen Howland. "Business leads to more business. Work, on the other hand, just keeps you away from business." In other words, work that will not further your business goals is undesirable. Business not only takes you farther on the road to success, but it keeps coming back to you in other ways. When you have good clients, they continue to bring even more business to you.

How do you get business, as opposed to work? Never lose sight of your goals, keep them firm in your mind and focus everything you do on that vision. It's just that simple. If you learn the basic tools for effective advertising and marketing, success will come to you faster.

# Focus, focus, focus

You already know what your specialty or specialties are. Now your job is to determine how best to reach the customers who want you to provide those services.

Obviously, if you make couture custom bridal gowns, setting out your business cards at the local sports bar or restaurant is going to net little return. However, if one of your services is sewing tackle twill on team jackets, that is a great way to get the word out about your business. Sponsoring a kids' soccer team could be a terrific use of your advertising dollars. For bridal experts, having a booth at the annual bridal show would be a much better use of your money, netting customers you might not have access to otherwise.

# Tell everyone about your business

When beginning a business, it's a good idea to let everyone know what you are doing. Wait, however, until your plans are ready to be put into action; it dissipates your energy to tell others too soon. Sometimes significant others are threatened by your dreams; in cases like this, it is often better to present an accomplished feat, rather than a pie in the sky plan for "someday."

Regardless of what you do, everyone knows someone who needs, or will need, your service someday. From the beginning, set up a way to reward and thank anyone who sends referrals your way. There are pre-printed thank-you cards with slots for business cards—this is a gracious way to show your gratitude. Include a card or two for your friend to pass along another time. Always say thank you, no matter how small the job that results from the referral. As a former boss always said, "You can't thank someone too often."

Learn, too, to ask for referrals from your satisfied clients. Some dressmaking customers are reluctant to refer their friends to their custom clothier. If you find this to be true, gently remind them that you need a certain number of good customers to stay in business. It is actually in their best interest that they send other people in need of your services to your studio. A steady clientele helps to even out the normal cycle of demand, too, and will help keep you from getting busy with other kinds of work in those slow times.

And remember: One satisfied customer will tell three people about the service you provided. One unhappy client will tell twenty others about the poor treatment he received from you. Always treat your customers as you would like them to portray you to their friends.

## A word about specializing

Many sewing business owners find that after their initial marketing push they don't need to advertise further. In some communities certain specialties are in such demand that there is little need to do much more than put a sign out front that says what you do. Your market research lays the foundation for this kind of success; if you have identified a market no one else is serving, you may find instant success.

# Inexpensive advertising

## Business cards

A box of business cards is just about the least expensive advertising you can purchase. However, they won't help you if you leave them in the box.

Double-sided business card

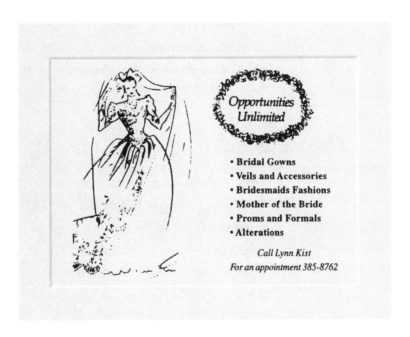

Opportunities Unlimited

• Bridal Gowns
• Veils and Accessories
• Bridesmaids Fashions
• Mother of the Bride
• Proms and Formals
• Alterations

*Call Lynn Kist*
*For an appointment 385-8762*

Invitation-style business card

Give them to everyone, even if the people you're handing them to don't seem likely to become customers. People tend to keep business cards, and they often pass them on to others. Also, restaurants, dry cleaners and other local businesses may have someplace to post your business card. Be careful about this, however; if your business card has your address on it, decide whether or not it is safe to leave your card out for anyone to see. You may want to design your card to have only your name and business name, a phone number and the words *By appointment only*.

Creativity counts in creative businesses. One of my favorite business cards sports a gold embossed needle with an actual golden thread dangling from its eye. Dee McCarthy has another cleverly designed card; it is double-sided, advertising two different specialties, in different but related color schemes. One retail and custom bridal shop uses a business card that resembles a wedding invitation.

# Bulletins

An inexpensive and relatively effective way to advertise many kinds of sewing businesses is through church and school bulletins. Your community offers many such opportunities. While waiting for church to begin, or while thumbing through a school program at intermission, readers are a captive audience. Make your ad eye-catching enough that it isn't passed over; give the readers an amusing or interesting diversion from their boredom.

# Press releases

Send press releases to your local newspapers announcing the opening of your new business. Whenever you change your business in any way, send a press release to the business editor or the fashion editor of the paper, whichever is more appropriate. This is most effective when the local paper is small, or if your community has weekly newspapers. Smaller papers are more willing to report news of this nature.

# Flyers

Flyers are great to let potential customers know about your business. Kim Lawrence, who lives near Williamsburg, left colorful flyers about her window treatment business in the news boxes of newer suburban homes. She chose to target an area of more affluent homeowners, who could afford to have custom treatments made for their newer homes. Note: If you decide to distribute flyers, do not leave them in mailboxes. In the United States, this is a federal offense—the interior of a mailbox is considered government property. Doorknob hangers also work well, and blank, computer printable hangers are available from paper companies and office supply stores.

If you choose to mail flyers, pick the recipients judiciously, and don't waste time or money sending flyers to people who have no need for your services. While mailings used to be fairly cheap, today's costs are considerably higher. At three stamps for a dollar plus copy costs, mailing can be more expensive than other ways of promoting your business, depending on how much return you expect.

Test your mailing piece for its effectiveness before committing to a large mailing. Ask everyone who calls you for business where they found out about your services, and keep a record of their answers. Also, consider sending out mail promotions a few at a time. Unless you qualify for a second-class bulk mailing permit, it makes more sense to spread out the work, the expense and the results. If you work alone, it might be best to bring in business a little at a time, rather than to be swamped with new customers all at once. People move occasionally; if you plan to use a mailing list more than once, be sure to record any changes in address.

# Newsletters

Newsletters can be a terrific way of building certain types of businesses. For instance, drapery workroom owners who send out monthly newsletters with decorating ideas can spur their customers to add to their existing decor. Sewing teachers can let their students and prospective students know about new classes being offered. Wearable artists and crafters can send out periodic newsletters to tell past customers where the artist's next craft show will be. This is an excellent way to boost business for shows; selling to someone you've already sold to is much easier than breaking new ground. This is especially effective if you have garments or decorative pieces that go with or coordinate with things these customers have already bought from you.

## Classified ads

Classified ads work better than display ads, for the amount of money that is spent. Use display ads later, when your business is able to pay for them. Classified ads are less costly, by far, and offer a better return on your dollar when your business is new.

## Signs

Signs in public places work in certain situations but not others. When you're just getting started, it is helpful to let as many people as possible know what you're doing, but some business isn't worth getting. First, consider your personal safety. Do you want just anyone calling you? If not, the signboard at the grocery store may not be the best place to advertise. Or simply word the sign carefully to reflect a phone number and your specialty only. In some smaller communities, this isn't a problem, but if you live in a large, impersonal city, do be careful. A sign advertising sewing classes at the neighborhood fabric store doesn't need anything but your name and a telephone number.

# Specialty advertising

Certain specialties have unique advertising and marketing possibilities. Targeting your efforts to get your business known makes sense.

## Alterations

Contact dry cleaners, ready-to-wear stores, bridal stores and tuxedo rental stores. If you don't do any custom sewing and another sewing professional does no alterations, consider sharing business with that person, referring one another to clients who ask for services you don't provide.

## Custom clothing

Contact ready-to-wear stores, bridal stores and fabric stores. Press releases to local newspapers help spark business. Consider writing a column for one of the community papers—a column on wedding tips, for instance, or coordinating clothing. Many custom clothiers also do color and wardrobe consulting. This is a wonderful way to introduce yourself to business-people, who have more need for well-fitting, good-looking clothing. Share marketing efforts with another compatible business in your area. If you do tailoring, consider sharing mailing costs with someone who does only alterations. Send out coupons for small discounts to members of the local Chamber of Commerce, for instance.

A note about marketing through fabric stores: This is a good way to get started, but you may not want to continue to get customers this way once your business is established. Fabric store customers tend to be in search of bargains, and in general, custom sewing should cost *more* than ready-to-wear, not less.

## Bridal

Many bridal designers began by doing one wedding for a friend, and some have grown their businesses by making wedding gowns for former bridesmaids for whom they had made gowns. Another way to find customers is to have a relationship with retail bridal stores. For those able to create similar styles in larger sizes, many bridal shops refer customers when they can't provide gowns in the right size. If you specialize in bridal alterations, contact the local bridal store. Bridal consultants are happy to refer their customers to both designers and makers of bridal accessories, such as wedding album covers and rice bags. Be aware that many dress-makers and other sewing pros will not make wedding gowns; this is another reason to network with other professionals.

## Window treatments, home decor items

Leave your business cards at fabric stores, especially any store in your area that specializes in home decorating fabrics. If you want to work with interior decorators, make appointments with three or four who do the kind of work you also like to do. Ask for a few minutes of their time, and take a portfolio of your work with you, even if the photos are of drapes or other items you made for your own home. (But don't tell them so, if this is the case!) Painters can also give you referrals, and real estate agents are wonderful contacts for locating new homeowners.

# Quilts

If you prefer to make quilts on a commission basis, your local quilt store will be an excellent place to make friends. Quality workmanship is hard to find, despite the number of quilters. Many hobby quilters only enjoy the piecework aspect of quilting; these people often have piles of finished tops that need hand or machine quilting. Other outlets for finding custom quilt work: antique stores (also a good place to find restoration clients), interior designers, specialty gift shops.

# Doll clothing, other hobby specialties

Find out where the local hobbyists meet, and make it a point to join them. Don't be shy about showing samples of your work; if this is your target market, make the most of any association with this group of potential buyers.

# Baby items

Leave flyers at pediatricians' offices, day care centers and churches.

# Crafts

Craft malls are great places to sell your work, especially if you don't have the time to sit at craft shows for weekends on end. Small booths are rented by the month, and the craft mall management retains a small percentage of the booth's income. This allows the craft producer to test different styles or products and is a great way to get started in part-time manufacturing and sales.

Craft shows reflect varying degrees of professionalism. At the bottom of the heap are table shows at schools and other nonprofit institutions. These venues usually have a small table rental fee, some as low as $15 for two days. With fees like this, your only other costs are for supplies to create the craft items and transportation to and from the show.

Larger craft shows, with much higher fees, are sometimes juried, or judged ahead of time. This ensures the participants that their products won't compete with others that may not be handmade and that several of the booths aren't carrying nearly identical products. It also maintains the quality of the booth offerings. This keeps customers coming back to juried shows, year after year. These shows also have a much higher booth or entrance fee.

If you decide to participate in a juried show, the promoters will want to see slides of your work. Photograph your work (with slide film) against a plain background for better visibility. (For more on selling crafts, see the references in the appendix.)

## Specialty products

Many products—parachutes, hot-air balloons, riding clothing, skiwear and kites, for instance—have ready-made sales outlets in the form of specialty magazines and newsletters. If you have writing talents, articles in such publications are an inexpensive way to promote your specialty. Press releases to these magazines are another way to advertise new versions of your product. Send press releases to the editor listed on the masthead at the front of the magazine. Other advertising may also be available, depending on the publication, for true target marketing. If there are trade associations in your field, find out if they accept advertising in their newsletters. For a fairly complete listing of trade associations and industry publications, consult your local library.

# Pricier advertising outlets

## Display ads

Display ads are among the most expensive of all advertising methods. These ads are the ones you see in newspapers and magazines, anything more than the simple classified ad. When you are just getting started, it is tempting to spend a lot of money on this kind of advertising, but avoid doing so. Unless your service depends heavily on foot traffic, many of the previously described methods will have a stronger impact on your business, without draining your budget. That said, display ads do have their place. For instance, if you have a commercial embroidery business and one of your new products is tied in with a major event in your city,

121

a display ad may generate enough business to pay for the ad and more. Not only that, it could lead to other more lucrative work. If you are announcing a sale, this is another time for a small display ad. Be judicious in planning these, however.

Beth Hodges of Virginia uses display ads to great advantage. Her window treatment business is long established, so she adds photos of jobs she has done to her ads to make them more appealing. Because she lives in a small town with a weekly newspaper, her advertising costs are low, and she has the benefit of more visibility. Readers look for her ad each week and try to guess whose house is being featured.

Marketing to a broader market means display ads in major publications. Many magazines offer discounts for first-time advertisers, and some even offer assistance creating the ad. If you want to inquire about rates, call the number listed under *Advertising* on the magazine's masthead.

## Yellow pages ads and listings

Any business on the street, that is, a freestanding shop, should have a yellow pages listing for its phone number. Display ads in the phone book can be expensive, so weigh the need for such expense carefully. If your business depends on customers finding you, look into listings under more than one heading, for example, *Dressmaking, Tailoring, Alterations* and any other related topics. Note: In the past, some phone companies insisted that all businesses, including home-based businesses, have business phone lines (which are more expensive than home lines). Find out what the local service provider requires for your business.

## Mass mailings

Mass mailings offer good exposure for some kinds of sewing businesses, especially those with manufactured products, such as specialty stuffed toys, custom furniture covers, kites or other sewn products. Access to a list of some kind will help you target your mailing efforts. Many trade, professional and consumer associations rent the lists of their members and may even proffer them on preprinted labels. A set amount per name, sometimes as little as $.10, is charged, with the understanding that this allows the renter to mail to these names one time only. Very often, dummy names are included in the list as a check to be sure the list isn't abused.

Barbara Shelton's banner

# Portfolios

Many types of sewing services are easier to sell if there is some kind of visual sales aid. A portfolio is helpful to bridal, window treatment and other home decor, crafts, dressmaking and many other kinds of businesses.

Barb Shelton of Milford, Ohio, has a bulging portfolio containing hundreds of drum corps banner styles created by her company, Banners by Barbara over the last fifteen years. Schools choosing from existing styles, for which she has already made patterns, save money on their total field banner costs.

When another designer has a new skating client, a flip through her portfolio is often enough to give the skater an idea of how his new costume should look. Photos are great aids for customers who have difficulty articulating what they want—they can merely point to photos that come close to the designs they have in mind. Window treatment photos offer this same advantage in client communication.

In order to create an effective and attractive portfolio, first choose a place to take the photo. Barb Shelton reserves one section of her studio wall as a photographic gallery, and she pins one of each of her original banners there for a portrait before it leaves the shop. If special banners are too large for the wall, they are photographed outdoors against a backdrop of greenery. The background should be as uncluttered as possible, with the focus totally on the item photographed.

In the case of bridal gowns, the best photos are those taken by the professional at the wedding. These are sometimes difficult to get, though. Your relationship with the bride often ends when you turn over the gown, unless you make an extreme effort to keep in touch. Some bridal designers make a point of attending the wedding, if possible, just to take their own pictures. Be sure to clear this with the bride ahead of time.

# Image

Whatever method you choose to promote your business, always be aware that the "medium is the message." In other words, be careful to portray yourself in as businesslike a fashion as possible. A flyer that is no more than a smudged photocopy with lots of typos won't make as good of an impression as one that is well thought out, spell-checked, and copied or printed onto clean, nicely folded paper. The difference in cost is slight; the difference in presentation is massive.

Another image maker or breaker is business stationery. Type the form on a self-correcting electronic typewriter (an inexpensive addition to your office), and photocopy the original; or, better yet, print a new contract or quote each time on your computer (see chapter ten).

Business cards are cheap; some office superstores print one thousand for under $30. Business cards can do double duty as hangtags for many sewn products until you get the capital to purchase your own labels. When you are ready to have labels made, many companies can design and produce them in a variety of quantities, from just one hundred to many thousands. Having your own label sewn into customers' garments adds another value-added quality in their eyes.

Professional-looking portfolios can be found at art stores; these make wonderful arty additions to your workplace. Some sewing pros prefer to use smaller photo albums. Home decor specialists, especially, benefit from toting idea books to clients' homes.

# CHAPTER 9

# Using Computers

Today's homes are more likely to include a personal computer than not. If you have one, consider using it to help make your sewing business more professional, more efficient and more profitable. If you don't have a computer yet, you might decide you want one after you read this chapter!

In the early 1980s, when personal computers were fairly new on the scene, the choices available were limited, not only for computers but also for software and accessories. My first system was ridiculously expensive for what it included: a monochrome (green screen) monitor; a very slow processor; and an enormous, incredibly slow and loud printer. I was pretty excited that I had the luxury of having two floppy drives (5¼-inch at the time), but there was no hard drive. To use my limited software applications, I had to memorize dozens of keyboard combinations. If I needed to print anything, I had to start it just before I went to lunch so I didn't waste all day waiting for one letter to finish printing. All these wonderful features were a rare bargain at $5,000. Yikes.

Things have certainly changed. Now even inexpensive computer systems include all kinds of goodies, and the system is ready to use right out of the box, to streamline your daily work and play activities. Not only that, but the learning curve has been shortened drastically by user-friendly programs that literally teach as you work.

A typical late-1990s system includes a color monitor, a hard drive capable of storing dozens of bookshelves worth of information, a fax modem that can answer the telephone, swift processors capable of performing multiple tasks in moments and CD-ROM drives. Massive programs that once would have required the use of many diskettes are now stored on one CD-ROM, including entire encyclopedias. Not only can you now use the CD-ROM drive to access this information, but you can also play music from your favorite music CDs while you work. By the time you read this book, more incredible advances may have been made; the technology is doubling in less than twelve months at this point.

So what does all this technological wonder have to do with a sewing business? It could have much to do with it, making your business more efficient than you ever dreamed it could be.

# "Works" packages

When you buy a new computer, it usually comes preloaded with software of a wide variety, some task oriented and some geared more toward entertainment. If you don't like what you get, it is a simple matter to uninstall one program and install another that you purchase.

There is typically an office suite, or "works," package installed. These packages enable you to perform a variety of office duties: composing letters, proposals, invoices and other written pieces; printing special envelopes; compiling address and other databases; developing spreadsheets (to create your own accounting program, if you desire); tracking appointments; designing newsletters, ads and flyers.

Some of the more common packages you will find: Microsoft Office, Corel WordPerfect, Microsoft Works (which is a less powerful home/office version of Microsoft Office) and Lotus Smart Suite. Any of these packages will help you do nearly everything in this chapter, except faxing, accounting, filling out tax returns and patternmaking.

# Business cards and letterhead

With the availability of many new printer-ready papers, almost anyone can create business cards. This is especially handy if you want to have a variety of cards to reflect different aspects of your business. For instance, if you alter bridal gowns and also make lacy doll clothes, you won't necessarily want both your specialties on the same card. Also, if you travel with the doll clothing part of the business, it might be more important to have the area code of your phone number on that card. Suppose you just want to try out a new specialty; the ability to print just a few cards gives you the flexibility to change your mind if things don't work out.

Most sewing businesses do not need the amount of preprinted stationery that comes in a minimum order. Not only do most of the word processing programs allow for making your own letterhead, but you can change it at a whim. Paper supplies represent a large investment if they are printed by a print shop; printing your own saves money, time and space. Moreover, it isn't wasted if information changes because you don't have to purchase a large quantity.

Flyers are easily created on computers, and mailing programs allow for efficient mailings. Using your customer database, you can readily inform your clients of any new and exciting changes in your business. Database labels are a snap to print with today's software and printers.

Policy sheets and price lists created on the computer are not only simpler to print than typed lists, they are also easy to change when it is time to raise prices or make additions. Each printed sheet is an original; no messy photocopies are necessary, nor is a trip to the copy shop. I recommend printing small amounts at a time. This reduces your commitment to prices and policies, as well as saves money on supplies.

Also available are cards to use as thank-you notes, referral cards, reminder cards and other promotional and customer service aids. Create your own logo, and repeat it on all your correspondence and marketing papers.

Develop forms for gathering customer information, then input the data into the computer. This also gives you a "track to run on" when asking questions—with a form to check, you don't forget to ask the right ones. (See appendix for templates for contracts and policy sheets.)

Laser printers are much less expensive than they were even a few years ago (and unheard of before then for home or office use). They make your printed materials look fabulous and can save you hundreds of dollars. And the most important benefit: Using your own professional-quality printer forms brings instant credibility to your business and makes you look like the pro you are!

# Bookkeeping, tax records, filing taxes

One of the most compelling reasons for keeping books in the first place is to determine your tax liability at year's end. With this in mind, it makes sense to consider a bookkeeping system that works with a tax-filing package. Today's computer programs offer a variety of flexible systems that work together.

Computer programs like this are simple to understand. Many bookkeeping programs work just like a checkbook: You simply fill in a check on-screen, and the data goes into an electronic "checkbook" file. You can even have checks printed from an ink jet or laser printer. For those who detest writing checks, this is a tremendous time-saver. In addition, the computer never makes addition mistakes, and as long as you keep transactions up-to-date, your checking account balance should be correct.

You can code every transaction that has anything to do with your business. Reports on how much was spent and collected in the business are simple to create. This makes it apparent right away if expenses need to be restrained or if a celebration is in order. Another tremendous benefit to the self-employed in the United States is the ability to see when your required quarterly estimated tax payment needs to be adjusted. Waiting until January to add up all the income and expenses could be a mistake; if you experience terrific income, you may end up owing more than you expected. And with that last quarterly payment due only three weeks after the holidays, that could be a hardship to someone who thought he had lots of extra cash that year.

Need a financial statement for a loan, or for your business plan? Most of the personal accounting programs have a preset financial statement template. Choose this from the menu of options, and a statement is printed immediately. These programs can also serve as training for more complex accounting packages.

In addition to the checking account programs such as Quicken and Microsoft Money, there are also several bookkeeping programs that allow you to create and track invoices, pay bills and even keep track of payroll and inventory. Some of the programs currently on the market include QuickBooks, Peachtree Accounting, M.Y.O.B. (Mind Your Own Business) and One-Write Accounting. In varying degrees of ease of use, these programs offer traditional accounting capabilities.

Most of these accounting programs are capable of keeping track of cost by project. This could be extremely beneficial to your business, especially if you find yourself making unplanned expenditures for jobs that seem to lose money instead of the other way around. Simply code each expense to track which job it belongs to.

## Tax packages

With two sole proprietors in my family, our taxes are a little complicated. For years I gave figures to our accountant, who then just filled in our return. Since I had been doing all the work anyway, I tried using one of the tax packages. It cost $40 and the accountant cost $300—a no-brainer, we decided. We were audited a couple of years ago, with no problems. The auditor told me the IRS feels that people who are conscientious enough to use computer bookkeeping and tax programs are usually honest—an added benefit!

Many tax packages provide a transfer utility that simply picks up any coded items from the bookkeeping package and merges them directly into the tax forms. However, you have to make sure your checking account or bookkeeping system has the correct coding. Returns are printed just as they would be if you filled them in by hand, only much neater.

There are several tax packages, including TurboTax, MacInTax and U.S. Tax. Because of the annual changes in the Internal Revenue Service tax code, it is important to use only the program meant for the tax year you are working on. Many of the companies that produce these programs offer a guarantee that they will support any errors their program contains. However, they won't support any data input errors you commit.

One caution about using these wonderful cyber helpers: They do not take the place of an accountant. You should still check to see what kinds of records for expenses and income to keep and which deductions to take. Many accountants can give advice about which program will work best for your business. However, once you are on your way, filling out and filing your own taxes can reflect tremendous savings.

# Inventory control and management

How many times has this happened: While at the fabric store, you pick up a couple things you need, only to find you already picked them up the last time you shopped. You might use them soon, but more likely that money could be used more productively elsewhere. However, it isn't always convenient to trudge back to the store to return the items.

This situation can be avoided with inventory control maintained in the computer. Most office packages have database programs included, or they can be purchased separately. Some of the most popular programs are Access, Lotus 1-2-3, ACT! and Quattro Pro. In addition, Success Publishing has developed a database program exclusively for sewing items, S.O.S., Sewer's Organization Software. These programs offer a way to record use and purchases of various inventory items: threads, interfacings, fabrics, notions, patterns, books, videotapes, machine maintenance records and much more.

# Customer records

Those same database programs can be used to keep tabs on customers. Names, addresses, phone numbers, sizes, color preferences and measurements can all be stored in alphabetical order with little effort on your part. If you don't want the expense of a major database program, there are several nifty little personal information manager (PIM) programs for storing these records and tracking your daily appointments. Sidekick, Outlook, Lotus Organizer and Janna Contact Personal are examples of programs currently available.

# Business plan

If you want to present your business plan to a bank, sometimes a little more "curb appeal" is necessary. The same process we walked through in chapter seven can be presented in a more appealing format with business plan software, or with a template in an office program. Lotus Smart Suite's Freelance Graphics contains a template with preset headings for a business plan presentation, among others. But even if you don't have special software, most word processing programs today are capable of producing larger fonts and boxes. Transfer the numbers and other information from your notes to a file you create for a more professional-looking presentation.

# Telephone and fax machines

Nearly every computer system sold today includes a fax modem capable of sending and receiving faxes. Many systems also include what is called telephony support, which basically serves as a sophisticated answering machine.

Unattended, the computer can answer the call with your voice or with a preset announcement and either send the call to a "mailbox" or receive a fax. If you have caller identification on that phone number, you can even see who is calling, right on the computer screen. Many programs have a feature that lets you preset certain favorite phone numbers—when those people call, a special screen pops up to alert you.

Hands-free phone calling is also possible. Most computers have speakers attached, and a microphone is often included as well. Since every computer now has jacks for headsets, simply hooking up the inexpensive headset to the computer affords a much less stressful way to hold a phone conversation, and provides privacy. (This assumes that the computer is fairly close to the sewing machines.)

Any document created in the computer can be faxed directly from the computer, without first printing the document. This comes in handy when sending credit references to suppliers, for example. Most companies today have fax machines, and it looks more professional to have your own fax number on a letterhead or business card. The ability to fax from your office also saves time and money if your other alternative is to run down the street to do it.

# Online access

The marvel of the twentieth century is the unlimited access to nearly anything in the world, right from your desk. Every day more businesses enter the worldwide marketing arena of the World Wide Web, which is only accessible by computer modem. This electronic world is populated by millions of content providers, many of them offering either items for sale or educational information. This information explosion is a boon to any business, but for sewing businesses in particular. Resources that were previously almost impossible to find are now accessible in moments.

E-mail offers immediate communication for keeping in touch with resources, other professionals and even customers. With an Internet access account, the solitude of owning a small business need not be as harsh a reality as it once was. Several online support groups have sprung up, which offer peer counseling and assistance in a matter of hours. Message boards on various online services and Internet newsgroups are available for a variety of special interest areas, including sewing and business. On-line chats offer a way to "talk" to others of like mind. Read and type responses to others from around the country and around the world.

The Internet and the online world are a rich source of information, assistance and networking for anyone. The sewing professional has much to gain by tapping into this vast wonderland in cyberspace. As of this writing, a search for the word *sewing* might net more than twenty thousand references. By the time you read this, that figure could nearly double, given the intense growth this medium is experiencing. Don't be left behind.

# Patternmaking software

For many dressmakers, new patternmaking software programs have been a boon to their businesses. Packages of varying degrees of complexity allow the custom clothier to create patterns to fit the unique measurements of individual customers.

There are pattern programs for the most rudimentary styles up to very sophisticated packages that allow grading for multiple sizes and layouts for hundreds of yards of fabric. In order to run the most sophisticated programs, more equipment is necessary; the simpler packages print on less expensive printers and run on more basic systems.

There are many ways to compare these programs, but such research will require some detective work on your part. Online services and Internet newsgroups are one outlet to find others who have used various systems; be aware that there is a wide variance of experience levels represented in such forums.

Lisa Shanley, a former professor at Auburn University, created the program Symmetry for use with home computers. This program allows for three levels of usage: creating custom slopers and applying a bank of patterns to them, creating your own patterns, and grading multiple sizes from your patterns. Lisa's company, Wild Ginger Software, also sells plotters for printing patterns for mass-produced garments. In the past, software packages of this kind would have cost tens of thousands of dollars; Symmetry is available in three price levels, the highest priced choice well under $1,000. This revolutionary shift in cost makes such technology available even to very small manufacturing businesses.

If you don't need to grade for multiple sizes, one of the other pattern drawing programs will suffice. (See the appendix for more information about software programs for patternmaking.)

Storage of professional patterns

# Choosing a computer

Don't just buy a computer you see advertised in Sunday's paper because it fits your price range; you may be seriously disappointed later. Research what you need and how powerful of a system is necessary to fill those requirements. Change is the most constant factor in the computer field, and you don't want to find that you outgrew your system before you even learned to make it work for you.

Fortunately there's a wealth of information about computers today. Any library or bookstore has literally hundreds of books on subjects from the very basics of what a computer is to getting the most out of various programs.

There are also many magazines on computing, at many different levels of expertise; one of my favorites is *Home Office Computing*. These

# Paul and Lisa Shanley

Aegis Design Group/BMFI/
Wild Ginger Software
Old Hickory, Tennessee

Having long-held interests in both clothing construction and outer space, it was a natural for Paul Shanley to apply his knowledge in both areas to developing protective clothing for the aerospace and aeronautics industries.

After three years at Auburn University (including three quarters in clothing design), Paul left school. He went to work as an apprentice in a costume design studio near Miami for seven months. His next job was as a counselor at NASA Space Camp in Huntsville, Alabama. After a couple of years of steeping himself in the space culture and lore, Paul went back to Auburn for a degree in speech communication, with the goal of working in aerospace and aviation public relations.

In 1989, shortly before the end of his degree program, Paul met Dr. Lisa Christman, a professor at the university. Lisa was preparing a proposal to work as a general contractor on a prototype for a Navy flight suit. This contract was based on fiber technology for flame resistance (FR fiber technology), and Lisa invited Paul to help on the project. When the thirty-day proposal project was over, Lisa and Paul began dating. Shortly afterward, they began a business together, called Aegis Design Group. *Aegis* means shield, or protection. This company created "cut and sew" protective clothing prototypes and product development for military and industry use.

As a professor, Lisa, who by now was

Dr. Lisa Shanley, was encouraged to pursue outside contracts. Together, Paul and Lisa became outside consultants to Dow Chemical Company, for whom they did several prototype projects, including putting an insulation fiber into ski jackets and cold weather sleeping bags. In addition, Lisa won a postdoctoral Navy engineering fellowship to do research. They worked on "end product user" protective equipment for soldiers and Marines. They developed a portable climate control simulator suit. Paul calls this "a poor man's heat chamber." It would allow the military to test potential fighter pilots to see their susceptibility to temperature extremes.

During a sabbatical from Auburn University, Lisa invented Symmetry, her patternmaking software, and she and Paul formed Wild Ginger Software, along with Diane Koza, Ph.D., another Auburn professor. Symmetry was the first computer program of this type to offer pattern grading in an affordable package, which allows even small manufacturers to create their own patterns and grade them.

In the meantime, Paul joined the National Guard and is now an end user of the kind of equipment he's been working on. In addition, he has formed a partnership, BMFI, with an inventor. This partner has developed FR fiber technology and an advanced type of insulation, both of which they intend to develop further and market to industry.

publications rate various kinds of hardware (the actual computer and peripheral equipment) and software (programs) and contain great business articles. You can learn a lot from the ads in these magazines, too, sometimes enough to know what questions to ask.

Check your local community education schedule or the computer store in your area for classes. Not only are the classes themselves valuable, but talking at the break or after class with other students can be very enlightening. Find out what they know and where they shop for their systems and programs. While you're at the computer store, browse the aisles to see what types of products they offer. This research time will pay for itself—promise!

# CHAPTER 10

# The Importance of Networking and Education

Over the years, my career in the sewing industry has progressed rapidly, in large measure due to networking with other professionals in sewing businesses. Without the many wonderful friends and contacts I've made in this fascinating field, I would not have had the courage to believe in myself enough to teach sewing, nor would I have ever written even one book. I really owe a great deal to my fellow Professional Sewing Association members here in Cincinnati. Hopefully, they have benefited equally by their friendships with me.

Today there are more opportunities for networking with other sewing professionals than ever before. Since the early 1980s, several professional groups have sprung up, offering many meeting and seminar options. (See the appendix for specific groups that may pertain to your specialty, as well as more general associations in the sewing for profit arena.)

The benefits of networking with your peers can't be stressed enough. Joining a group of other sewing professionals can make a difference to your business. Not only does it alleviate the loneliness of working solo, but it also helps to be able to compare notes about various aspects of business. Often, the problems you experience are the same ones others have had. It helps to know you aren't the only one who has gone through such situations. In addition, knowing that another business on the other side of town is able to charge double what you charge may help you increase your prices. Sharing wholesale sources and orders could be another benefit of working with other pros. And it pays to let others know you specialize in certain types of work; referrals from other professionals have lent a helping boost to many businesses.

Don't be afraid to join volunteer groups; these can be an excellent source of new clients. People you meet in support organizations for the arts, for instance, often need evening clothing. Builders associations are great resources for new home and commercial office construction needing window treatments or other sewn products. Church and school groups are other places to network with potential customers.

Even volunteering to sew something for a group can lead to new business. One woman made new cushion covers for the children's section of the local library. A small placard placed nearby announced her work. She received several calls within a few weeks from mothers who had enjoyed the attractive and comfortable new seating with their children and wanted the businessperson to do that quality of work for them. Another enterprising young man volunteered to make costumes for a theatre production benefit. His name in the program brought new customers to his door.

# Networking opportunities

## Association memberships

Professional associations also offer a way to share information with others. It is my considered opinion that no one has all the answers; we can learn a great deal from one another. Who better to learn from than someone who has been in business for awhile? Take a shortcut to success by taking advantage of others' hard-earned knowledge. However, even beginners often adapt new and creative solutions to common questions of technique. It is interesting to see how our different backgrounds help us arrive at different ways of dealing with the same thorny problems.

Another terrific benefit of getting to know other professionals in your area is that you eventually become familiar with one another's work. When a client or potential client asks for a service your business doesn't provide, having this knowledge of how well a colleague sews can reduce embarrassment in making referrals that turn out all wrong. Conversely, your associates are more willing to send business your way when they feel confident of *your* ability.

Joining such a group and attending meetings regularly can help you in many ways. Not only do you make valuable contacts, but most meetings have varying degrees of an educational aspect. Everyone has a slightly different approach to the way he does business, and getting a glimpse of another's methodology can forever change the way you see certain aspects of your business.

Many association members share information about problem customers, too. Forewarned is forearmed. Especially custom clothiers occasionally get hold of a live one: extremely difficult to fit, rude, picky, abusive and sometimes even scary. It certainly is comforting to members to find out they weren't the only ones to have problems with these individuals!

# Newsletters

One of the most tangible benefits of membership in a professional group is receiving the association newsletter. Keeping abreast of what other members are doing can give you something by which to measure your own success. Resources and techniques are often shared, as are details of what other local organizations are planning.

Here in Cincinnati the Professional Sewing Association (PSA) also keeps up with events hosted by the local Fashion Group International, the Women's Entrepreneurs group and a new organization of window treatment professionals. Attending these events offers even more chances for networking, but of an entirely different sort. Many of our members have made excellent contacts with professionals in other fields who need sewing services.

# Industry events

Also new in the last fifteen years or so are consumer sewing shows. These events are usually held at convention centers or hotels and offer a way to see many new industry products in one place. In addition, these shows feature many classes, seminars and free venues given by a variety of industry speakers. For the most part, these shows do not afford professional-level instruction. However, we are all on a journey through life, and not everyone is at the same stage of the trip. If your personal quest for information includes learning new information, any level is important to you.

For more business-specific instruction, there are several conventions each year that offer this higher level of information. For all kinds of sewing professionals, Beyond Pin Money: A Conference for Sewing Professionals, sponsored by the Cincinnati PSA, provides serious business help. The goal of Beyond Pin Money is to provide a variety of professional-level classes and a venue for networking with professionals from around the United States and Canada. Professional Association of Custom Clothiers (PACC) also sponsors a convention each year in conjunction with its annual meeting. Instruction at this event is geared more toward custom dressmaking. For tailors, the Custom Tailors and Designers Association of America (CTDA) also has a convention annually.

Drapery and window treatment workrooms are in the catbird seat; there are several events for this group, sponsored by the two industry magazines, *Draperies & Window Coverings* and *Window Fashions*. Technique seminars, business meetings and resource booths all appear at these events.

Quilt Market is for anyone in the quilt business, whether you quilt, write about quilting, sell quilt-related products or just want to find new products. This semiannual event is held in Texas and another part of the country each winter and summer.

The International Costumer's Guild, the Society for Creative Anachronism (SCA) and other groups hold costuming conventions around the country. Some of these are massive events, with seminars, product vendor arenas, contests and celebrity appearances. If your area of expertise is in any kind of reenactment or fantasy costuming, these are can't-miss shows.

Dollmakers and doll clothing makers should investigate the many hobby shows for dolls and the products that surround them. Many kinds of crafting are represented at shows presented by Hobby Industry Association of America (HIA), and the Association of Crafts & Creative Industries (ACCI).

For small manufacturers, the premier event is the Bobbin Show, held every fall in Atlanta, Georgia. At this enormous show, companies who sell products that support the sewing manufacturing business are represented. Here you will find everything from buttons to button sew machines, trims to trimmers, monograms to monogram machines. Quilting and embroidery machines are shown, from sizes to fit your basement to enormous machines more suited to traditional factories. Factory owners and small manufacturers alike attend this show, coming from all over the world. Listening in on passing conversations you are as likely to hear Polish as English, Chinese as Japanese, Portuguese as Spanish.

# Online chats and lists

The newest way to network is by plugging into the vast possibilities of the cyberworld. With a modem and an online service provider, such as America OnLine or another of the hundreds of companies that have sprung up in recent years, you can instantly access any of several business support systems.

One such group is the SewPros Network. Begun in December 1996, this group now has several hundred members from all over the world, with sewing businesses ranging from dressmakers to heirloom smockers to outerwear manufacturers. Monthly "chats" augment weekly e-mail digests and other benefits. The chats offer a way to "speak" to members immediately—if you can type, you can talk. You merely type what you want to say into a special block on the screen; when the *Enter* key is pressed, the text is presented to the chat group. Because of the immediacy of this medium, chat members are in all sorts of time zones and in a variety of geographic locations, but all are able to communicate at once.

In addition to SewPros, there are also networks and e-mail digests, or "lists," for drapery workrooms, childrenswear manufacturers and many other specialties (see the appendix).

Online message or bulletin boards are another way to network. In 1994 I conducted a survey of 540 sewing professionals; nearly 20 percent of those surveyed were people I had "met" on sewing message boards on Prodigy and America OnLine. Today that number would be much higher, as personal computers have become more commonplace and more affordable. Message boards offer a place to find out more—more about sources, more about techniques, more about what is happening outside your own four walls. The Internet also has bulletin boards, which are called newsgroups. There are two specifically for sewing:

- alt.sewing
- rec.crafts.textiles.sewing

Take a spin in cyberspace and you'll be amazed at the possibilities.

# Related nonsewing networking

Sometimes, the best contacts you can make are outside your own industry. Breakfast (or lunch or dinner) clubs set up to share leads with other professionals can offer ample opportunity for finding new customers. For instance, drapery and window treatment professionals who network with real estate professionals, interior decorators, builders and office managers are situated perfectly to make client contacts from among the clients of those other businesses. In the same way, tailors and custom clothiers find new customers when they attend Chamber of Commerce meetings or charity functions. Bridal designers can have carte blanche to the contacts made among florists, jewelers, formalwear rental outlets and event planners.

Create your own networking group; arrange a working breakfast twice a month for people you feel might help one another's business. Typically such a club has half a dozen or more members, each in a different but perhaps related industry. Weekly or monthly meetings to exchange marketing ideas and new contact names often lead to more business for each member. Share names, addresses, phone numbers and other pertinent information about clients. Make it clear that each meeting lasts no more than forty-five minutes, and each time, everyone must share at least as many names as there are members of the group. Be sure to find out as much as you can about each member's business, and keep up with new events planned by each company represented.

Another fabulous way to find clients is to hang out where they are. One woman did just this. She wanted to do custom dressmaking, specializing in formalwear and other fine clothing. In order to meet those who would eventually become her clients, she joined volunteer groups in the arts: Friends of the Ballet, the service arm of the symphony, the opera volunteers. She met the movers and shakers in the social scene in these groups. Whenever anyone asked her what she did, a business card was proffered, along with a description of her services. Kateri Ellison found that her membership in the Greater Washington (DC) Board of Trade was a natural source of new custom clothing clients. As a business group, members expect to network with one another, and they make a point of supporting one another.

# Educate yourself

Continuing education is mandatory in many fields, but in the sewing industry, we often have to motivate ourselves to continue to learn new things. In the last fifteen years or so, there have been more changes in our field than in the previous eighty years; many new techniques, products and machines have been developed. Taking the time to update your education will make your business more profitable.

## Ngai Kwan

Ngai Kwan Designs
Seattle, Washington

Ngai Kwan

Ngai Kwan worked in the sewing industry for awhile, but was disgruntled with her marketing choices. Wondering why nothing she wanted to make for herself was in the pattern books, she decided to take some classes in both patternmaking and design.

At Seattle Central Community College, Ngai enrolled in the Apparel Design and Services program. The sewing, pattern design and grading curriculum was very intense, more difficult than her bachelor degree. Instead of cramming three years of information into two years, which was normally done, Ngai decided to take three years to finish so she could concentrate on her studies better.

A talent for patternmaking led to a career choice: Ngai now creates patterns for local seamstresses. They give her the measurements of the clients on a form she provides, along with a sketch, then Ngai makes the pattern. She is paid by the job or by the hour; Ngai says experienced patternmakers can make up to about $25 an hour locally.

One of her clients is a Seattle bridal designer who makes about one hundred gowns a year and employs two other patternmakers. Ngai submits the pattern to the customer, along with a sample, then the client corrects the fit and returns it to Ngai to correct the pattern. For her bridal customer, she sends a muslin for the bride to OK, and fitting changes are transferred to the pattern, if necessary. Another client brought her this challenge: to make a pattern for a one-seam hooded robe for prizefighters. In order to manage the robe with one seam, certain fabric requirements had to be specified. Because of the massive necks and shoulders of fighters, this was a thorny problem to work out.

She feels her method of patternmaking from the client's measurements is faster than changing a pattern made from a sloper; it's also more accurate. Because older slopers are slightly oversized, Ngai says the newer, highly fitted styles are impossible to fit with them. With the oversized styles of the last decade, many industry patternmakers have lost the ability to fit the body more closely. Ngai recommends Helen Armstrong's book, *Patternmaking for Fashion Design*.

---

Not only are there new, speedier techniques, but there are new fibers on the market. Microfibers, Tencel, hemp and many stretch fabrics are all recent developments on the fabric scene. Learn about these products before you are called upon to use one of them in a project; by then it might be too late to get the information you need about handling it. In addition, being prepared means knowing in advance that a certain kind of machine foot or needle is needed; this reduces panic buying, which can cost more of your hard-earned profit.

It is equally important to keep up with fashion and trends. An entire line of kitchen accessories in last year's country colors that won't sell this year could keep your family supplied for the rest of your life. The latest looks in dance fashions are important to competitive dancers; your customers look to you for guidance in choosing styles and fabrications.

Another trend worth paying attention to is individual color analysis. Many custom clothiers offer their customers this service, along with wardrobe planning. Knowing the latest color theories and using them to help your clients could help fatten your bank balance.

# Degree programs

There are some fashion design and apparel technology programs in the United States, but few of these schools teach sewing. Many programs have changed from the traditional Home Economics degree programs, and often you have to create your own educational experience. Going to various conferences will help and, additionally, attending as many business seminars as possible. The Small Business Administration (SBA) offers seminars and ongoing classes in many areas of the country. Call the local office to see what classes are scheduled in your area.

Four-year degree programs rarely include the subject matter most germane to a custom sewing business. A better bet might be one of the many two-year programs around the country. Business courses are also offered at these schools, but not necessarily in the same program, though they are equally important. A good grounding in business basics is essential for business success, and you just can't have too much information in this area.

In order to teach sewing, it isn't necessary to have a degree in sewing, unless you plan to teach at an accredited school. However, for teaching at a retail store or in your own school, a love of sewing and a good knowledge of techniques, as well as good communication skills, are much more important than a degree.

# Specialty schools

Several schools exist for concentrated instruction in various aspects of sewing. Cheryl Strickland's drapery school offers classes in many different areas of home decor sewing for business. Palmer/Pletsch Associates in Portland, Oregon, has a widely known school for teaching various subjects, including teaching people to teach sewing. Susan Khalje has a bi-coastal school, teaching concentrated bridal and couture techniques in both Baltimore, Maryland, and Portland, Oregon.

# Susan Khalje

Couture Sewing School
Glen Arm, Maryland

Susan Khalje and Catherine Stephenson with the Bridal Sewing School

From concert pianist to couture sewing instructor, Susan Khalje has moved from one fine art to another. After a career as a concert pianist that found her living in London, Susan changed her focus and returned to the United States. She went to New York City and found a job as a seamstress with a couture house. Susan describes the experience as total immersion in the world of haute couture. In addition to sewing the house's own designs, Susan was also asked to work on copies of haute couture garments for many of the bluebloods and celebrities of New York City and the eastern seaboard. She says, "I worked on the best fabrics, with the finest techniques."

Susan went out on her own after about a year and a half, when she was asked to go to Afghanistan to run a sportswear clothing factory there. While in Afghanistan, Susan caught the eye of the factory owner's best friend, and she and Qadir Khalje married. They lived there for awhile until moving to Amsterdam and then to the United States

In the early 1980s, Susan wanted to get back into sewing—she had been away from her piano practice too long to play professionally—and wanted something that would be more amenable to raising children. Susan was featured in an article on dressmakers in a national magazine. Out of this Susan got a job making a wedding dress, which appealed to her sense of special sewing. She continued to make custom wedding gowns and evening wear for the next fifteen years. Self-taught in altering patterns and creating whatever needs to be made, Susan feels her strength is in technique.

The Bridal Sewing School began in October 1993. Susan has since changed the name to Couture Sewing School because, she says, "We're talking about couture treatments, for special garments. Bridal gowns just happen to be white and have a lot of lace. That requires a lot of special treatment. We're basically set up as a European couture atelier. The emphasis is on hand sewing, but they bring machines. Every morning we do couture samples." Susan finds it advantageous to have group classes. She explains, "The beauty of having group classes is that you may not be working on Alençon lace, but someone else might, and you get to see what techniques apply. You really apply your knowledge right away, which I think is the way to learn. My goal as a teacher is to teach them how to think about the decision-making process of sewing in this way and the solid reasoning behind various choices."

Many students bring a gown they're working on, often for a client. The cost, as this book is being written, is $895 tuition, plus hotel, food, airfare or other travel.

Susan says, "It's very difficult to get training at this level. If you want to use the finer techniques, where else can you go? Almost every other school is based on production sewing, except for a handful of classes here and there. I think the pendulum of higher sewing is swinging back, and couture is becoming a more recognized thing again." The desire to create, and to own, very fine things has begun to come back in certain areas.

Catherine Stephenson of Portland, Oregon, helps Susan in the classes. Catherine shares Susan's love of the couture methods, the fine hand sewing and attention to detail that earmark the most custom of garments.

Susan feels that teaching for several years has changed her focus and changed the way she communicates to her classes. She feels she has become more effective as a result of observing how different people respond to what she has to say. Some of her students put a lot of pressure on themselves to complete a garment during the six-day class, and she found that she had to be sensitive to the various goals of the students. For instance, her original advertising suggested that the class was for intermediate and advanced sewists; Susan has changed this to say "advanced and professional."

Susan was elected chairperson of PACC in 1996 for the first two-year term of the organization. Coincidentally, Catherine Stephenson will be her successor as chairperson in 1998.

# Sample Contract (For a Drapery Workroom)

**Your Company Name**
Your Company Address
City, State Zip/Postal Code
Phone/Fax Numbers

## Proposal and Acceptance

Submitted to: _____ Date: _____

Phone: Day _____ Evening _____

Billing Address: _____

Job Location: _____ Due Date: _____

**I hereby submit specifications and estimates for**

_____

_____

_____

_____

_____

_____

I propose hereby to furnish material and labor, complete in accordance with above specifications, for the sum of $ _____.

NOTE: This proposal may be withdrawn if not accepted within _____ days.

## Terms and Conditions:

1. Orders for articles, materials or contractor's services will not be placed in work until signed confirmation of PROPOSAL CONTRACT IS RECEIVED, together with any required deposit.
2. Prices of materials, articles and contractor's services are subject to change. Before proceeding with order, notice of any price increase will be given and confirmation of revised price required.
3. Prices do not included shipping, freight or trucking charges or insurance in transit, all of which will be at customer's expense.
4. Orders approved under this contract are noncancelable.
5. Prices do not include sales or other applicable taxes.
6. No responsibility is assumed for delays occasioned by failure of others to meet commitments or for any other reason or cause beyond our control.
7. Designs, samples, drawings and specifications shall remain Designer's property, whether or not the work for which they are made be executed.
8. Designer does not guarantee any fabric, material or article against wearing, fading or latent defect, but to extent permitted by law. Customer shall have benefit at customer's sole expense in the assertion thereof, of all guarantees and warranties possessed by the Designer against suppliers and manufacturers.
9. Furnishing or installing of any or all materials or articles is subject to Designer's ability to obtain the same and to procure the necessary labor thereof, and is contingent on strikes, accidents or other causes beyond Designer's control.
10. If Designer is required to render services not contemplated by this agreement, or incurs extra drafting or other expenses due to changes ordered by Customer for any other cause, Designer shall be paid for such extra services and expenses the reasonable value of cost thereof.
11. This contract is for custom-made products not subject to return.
12. Design changes, alterations and additions will be subject to further charges to Customer. Such changes, alterations and additions must be submitted in writing and agreed to and signed by both Designer and Customer. Additional deposit may be required.
13. PAYMENT TERMS: 50% Deposit required with all approved contracts. Balance is due on delivery of goods.

## ACCEPTANCE OF PROPOSAL:

The above prices, specifications, terms and conditions have been fully explained to me and are satisfactory. I hereby accept this proposal and authorize work to be done as specified. Payment will be noted as above.

Authorized Signature: _____ Date: _____

# Sample Contract (For a Custom or Bridal Clothing Business)

**Your Company Name**
Your Company Address
City, State Zip/Postal Code
Phone/Fax Numbers

Date: _____

Wedding/event date: _____

Estimated completion: _____

Policy sheet received: _____

Name: _____

Address: _____

Other: _____

Home Phone: _____

Work Phone: _____

Phone: _____

Description of gown or garment: _____

_____

_____

_____

Materials *(include yardage and estimated cost, if applicable):*

Fabric: _____

Fabric: _____

Lining: _____

Lace: _____

Lace: _____

Labor: _____

_____

_____

Beadwork: _____

_____

Payment schedule: _____

Materials: _____

Labor: _____

Subtotal: _____

Total: _____

| Date: | Amount: | Balance Due: |
|-------|---------|--------------|
|       |         |              |
|       |         |              |
|       |         |              |
|       |         |              |

Changes in weight or garment design may
necessitate additional charges. Payment in full
is required before release of this work.

X _____

X _____

*(Based on a form developed by Karen Howland.)*

# Policy Sheet (For a Custom Clothing Business)

**Your Company Name**
Your Company Address
City, State Zip/Postal Code
Phone/Fax Numbers

Thank you for choosing my company for your project; I look forward to working with you. I take great pride in the quality of my work for all my clients and in providing these services in a timely fashion. To accomplish these goals, I have established certain criteria:

- Clients are scheduled by appointment only. This ensures that all clients will have my undivided attention and will not be inconvenienced by waiting.
- I schedule only those projects that can be successfully completed in a given time period. This policy guarantees that all deadlines are met.
- Clients are asked to please call ahead to cancel appointments. Missed or tardy appointments, without notification, are subject to additional charges.

## TYPICAL PROJECT SCHEDULE

**Consultation:**
This is where we talk, bounce around wants, ideas, needs, desires and estimates, and determine if we should continue. All consultations are billed at the rate of $25 per hour, with a $25 minimum, and are due at the time of consultation. If we decide to work together on a project, the consultation fee is waived.

**Design Plan:**
At this time we nail down a definite design, determine materials and their purchase and formalize an agreement. Feel free to bring photos and/or patterns or a favorite garment to reproduce. They are extremely helpful in the design process. Please allow 4 to 8 weeks from consultation to final fitting. A 50% deposit on labor and the estimated cost of fabrics and notions are due at this time. These are nonrefundable.

**Fittings:**
Fittings are a required part of custom sewing. There can be anywhere from two to six fittings per item; three is customary. Come prepared with proper undergarments, shoes and any other accessories necessary for the finished garment, to ensure the perfect fit.

**Final Fitting:**
This is when we both determine that the fit is good, and all is well . . . at last! We will also "balance the books" at this time. Any credit for an overestimate on materials is applied and a final payment, in cash, is due.

## PLEASE REMEMBER:

We are working together. Workmanship only is guaranteed. The proposal you receive is for your weight and measurements as of _____ date. Finished work left for over 30-days is subject to storage fee. After 90 days, the articles will be sold. We pass on to you the $30 returned check fee our bank charges for any returned checks. No work will be released unless paid in full, including such charges. Extra charges may be required when measurements are obtained from an outside source and for fabric you provide. Any changes to the original contract will require additional charges. I understand the above policies:

Signed: _____ _____
CUSTOMER                                                                DATE

Signed: _____ _____
OWNER                                                                    DATE

# Appendix

## Professional Associations

**American Apparel Manufacturers Association (AAMA),** 2500 Wilson Blvd., Suite 301, Arlington, VA 22201, (800) 520-2262.

**American Home Sewing and Craft Association (HSA), International Sewing Machine Association (ISMA),** 1350 Broadway, Suite 1601, New York, NY 10018, (212) 714-1655.

**American Sewing Guild (ASG),** 9140 Ward Parkway, Suite 200, Kansas City, MO 64114, (816) 444-3500.

**Association of Crafts & Creative Industries (ACCI),** 1100-H Brandywine Blvd., P.O. Box 2188, Zanesville, OH 43702-2188, (614) 452-4541.

**Custom Tailors and Designers Association of America (CTDA),** 17 E. Forty-fifth St., New York, NY 10017, (212) 661-1960.

**Embroidery Trade Association International,** 745 N. Gilbert Rd., Suite 124-362, Gilbert, AZ 85234, (602) 497-1274.

**Fashion Group International, Inc.,** 597 Fifth Ave., New York, NY 10017.

**The Greater Columbia Fantasy Costumer's Guild,** P.O. Box 683, Columbia, MD 21045.

**Greater Metro Professional Sewing Association (GMPSA),** P.O. Box 23382, Richfield, MN 55423.

**Hobby Industry Association of America (HIA),** 319 E. Fifty-fourth St., P.O. Box 348, Elmwood Park, NJ 07407, (201) 794-1133.

**Industrial Fabrics Association International (IFAI),** 345 Cedar St., Suite 800, St. Paul, MN 55101-1088, (612) 222-2508.

**The International Costumer's Guild,** 1444 Arona St., St. Paul, MN 55108.

**Iowa Textile and Apparel Association,** % Textiles & Clothing Extension, 1055 LeBaron Hall, Iowa State University, Ames, IA 50011-1120, (515) 294-6712.

**National Association for Female Executives (NAFE),** 30 Irving Place, Fifth Floor, New York, NY 10003, (212) 477-2200.

**The National Needlework Association (TNNA),** P.O. Box 2188, Zanesville, OH 43702-2188, (203) 431-8226.

**Professional Association of Custom Clothiers (PACC),** P.O. Box 8071, Medford, OR 97504-0071, (541) 772-4119.

**Professional Dressmakers Association,** % Kim Baumunk-Kleine, Ultimate Stitch, Inc., 5401 Goethe Ave., St. Louis, MO 63109.

**Professional Needle Guild, Inc. (PNG),** P.O. Box 40236, Cleveland, OH
   44140.

**Professional Sewing Association of Ohio, Inc. (PSA),** % 944-B Sutton
   Rd., Cincinnati, OH 45230-2581.

**Rhode Island Home Sewing Network,** % Cheryl Lepore, 70 New
   Gardners Neck Rd., Swansea, MA 02777-2524.

**Window Coverings Association of America (WCAA),** 825 S. Waukegan
   Rd., Suite A8-111, Lake Forest, IL 60045-2665, (888) 298-WCAA.

# Resources

**Service Corps of Retired Executives (SCORE).** Call your nearest Small
   Business Administration office for information.

**Small Business Development Centers.** Call your local Chamber of
   Commerce to find the nearest one.

**State Extension Services.** Ask for their catalog of available publications.

## Schools

**Clemson Apparel Research,** Pendelton, SC, (864) 646-8454.

**Couture Sewing School,** 4600 Breidenbaugh Lane, Glen Arm, MD 21057,
   (410) 592-5711.

**Cheryl Strickland's Professional Drapery Workroom School,** P.O. Box
   867, Swannanoa, NC 28778, (800) 222-1415.

**TC$^2$,** Manufacturing Research Facility, Cary, NC.

**University of Rhode Island Cooperative Extension,** Woodward Hall,
   Kingston, RI 02881-0804, (401) 762-0960.

## Patternmaking software

**Dress Shop 2.5** Livingsoft, Inc., P.O. Box 819, Susanville, CA 96130-0819,
   (800) 626-1262.

**Fittingly Sew,** Knitcraft, 500 N. Dodgian Ave., Independence, MO 64050-
   3023, (816) 461-1217.

**Patternmaker Software,** 2029 144th Ave. SE, Bellevue, WA 98007-6216,
   (206) 644-8161.

**Personal Patterns,** Water Fountain Software, 13 E. Seventeenth St., Third
   Floor, New York, NY 10003, (212) 929-6204.

**Symmetry,** Wild Ginger Software, 4847 Mockingbird Lane, Old Hickory,
   TN 37138, (888) 929-9453.

## Patternmaking system

**Cut to the Fit,** Karen K. Howland, Kensinger Press, 1316 W. Pine St., Chillicothe, IL 61523, (309) 274-4160.

## Organization software

**S.O.S., Sewer's Organization Software,** Success Publishing, 5706 Edgepark Dr., Cleveland, OH 44142-1026, (216) 779-4844.

**Contract Forms, Price Lists, and Policy Sheets,** Sewstorm Publishing, 944 Sutton Rd., Cincinnati, OH 45230-3581, (513) 232-5403.

## Business consultants

**Karen Maslowski,** SewStorm, 944 Sutton Rd., Cincinnati, OH 45230-3581, (513) 232-5403. http://www.sewstorm.com

**Kitty Stein,** Workroom Concepts, P.O. Box 283, Clearbrook, VA 22624, (703) 667-5939.

## Supplies, including professional pressing equipment

**Atlanta Thread & Supply Corp.,** 695 Red Oak Rd., Stockbridge, GA 30281, (800) 331-7600, (770) 389-9115.

**Baer Fabrics,** 515 E. Market St., Louisville, KY 40202, (502) 569-7017.

**Banasch's Inc.,** 2810 Highland Ave., Cincinnati, OH 45212, (800) 543-0355.

**Brewer Sewing Supplies Co.,** 3800 W. Forty-second St., Chicago, IL 60632, (800) 444-3111, (773) 247-2121.

**Greenberg & Hammer, Inc.,** 24 W. Fifty-seventh St., New York, NY 10019-3918, (800) 955-5135, (212) 246-2836.

**B&G Lieberman Co.,** 2420 Distribution St., Charlotte, NC 28203, (800) 438-0346, (704) 376-0717.

**Sewing Emporium,** 1079 Third Ave., Chula Vista, CA 91911, (619) 420-3490.

**SouthStar Supply Co.,** 233 Oceola Ave., P.O. Box 90147, Nashville, TN 37209, (800) 288-6739, (615) 353-7000.

**3A Thread & Supply Co.,** 3216 N. San Gabriel Blvd., Rosemead, CA 91770, (818) 307-9705.

**Washington Millinery Supply Inc.,** P.O. Box 5718, Derwood, MD 20855, (301) 963-4444.

**Ely E. Yawitz Co.,** 1717 Olive St., Seventh Floor, P.O. Box 14325, St. Louis, MO 63103, (800) 325-7915, (314) 231-5729.

## Online resources—Web sites

**DraperyPros:** http://members.aol.com/garbarini/DraperyPro.html
**National Craft Association:** http://www.craftassoc.com
**SewPros Network:** http://www.sewstorm.com
**Thomas Register:** http://www.thomasregister.com
**TIMS (Textile, Apparel and Fashion Service):** http://www.unicate.com

## Periodicals

*The Crafts Report: The Business Journal for the Crafts Industry*, 300 Water St., P.O. Box 1992, Wilmington, DE 19899, (302) 656-2209.

*Draperies & Window Coverings*, Clark Publishing, 450 Skokie Blvd., Suite 407, Northbrook, IL 60062, (847) 498-9880.

*Embroidery Business News*, Virgo Publishing, Inc., 3300 N. Central Ave., Phoenix, AZ 85012-2501, (602) 990-1101.

*Embroidery/Monogram Business*, P.O. Box 1266, Skokie, IL 60076-8266, (214) 239-3060.

*The Independent Patternmaker*, 604 Forest Park Blvd., Fort Worth, TX 76102.

*Seamstress Network* (Drapery Workrooms), LaVelle Pinder Decorating, 9102 Collingwood Dr., Austin, TX 78748-6012, (512) 282-0717.

*SewWHAT? The International Newsletter for Professional Drapery Workrooms*, Cheryl Strickland, 101 Strickland Terrace, Swannanoa, NC 28778-2457, (888) 4SEWWHAT.

*Stitches: The Magazine for the Commercial Embroidery Industry*, Intertec Publishing Corporation, 9800 Metcalf Ave., Shawnee Mission, KS 66212-2216, (913) 341-1300.

*Window Fashions*, G&W McNamara Publishing, Inc., 4225 White Bear Pkwy., Suite 400, St. Paul, MN 55110, (612) 293-1544.

## Books

Brabec, Barbara. **Homemade Money.** Cincinnati: Betterway Books, 1997.

Caputo, Kathryn. **How to Start Making Money With Your Crafts.** Cincinnati: Betterway Books, 1995.

Duncan, Beth. **Sewing as a Business.** Meridian, Miss.: Mississippi Cooperative Extension Service, 1967.

Edwards, Paul, and Sarah Edwards. **Working From Home.** New York: Putnam, 1994.

Howland, Karen K. **Unit Pricing for Dressmaking.** Chillicothe, Il.: Kensinger Press, 1995.

Kishel, Gregory, and Patricia Kishel. **Start, Run, and Profit From Your Own Home-Based Business.** New York: John Wiley and Sons, Inc., 1991.

Levinson, Jay C., and Charles Rubin. **Guerrilla Selling.** Boston: Houghton Mifflin Company, 1992.

Long, Steve, and Cindy Long. **You Can Make Money From Your Arts and Crafts.** Scotts Valley, Calif.: Mark Publishing, 1988.

Maslowski, Karen L. **Sew up a Storm: All the Way to the Bank!** Cincinnati: SewStorm Publishing, 1995.

Ramsey, Dan. **The Crafter's Guide to Pricing Your Work.** Cincinnati: Betterway Books, 1997.

Roehr, Mary A. **Sewing as a Home Business.** Sedona, Ariz.: Mary Roehr Books and Video, 1996.

Shaeffer, Claire. **Price It Right.** Palm Springs, Calif.: La Mode Illustree, 1984.

Spike, Kathleen. **Sew to Success.** Portland, Ore.: Palmer/Pletsch Associates, 1990.

Sykes, Barbara Wright. **The "Business" of Sewing.** Chino Hills, Calif.: Collins Publications, 1992.

# Index